Moser Artistic Glass
Edition Two

Revised, Updated Edition of *Moser—Artistry in Glass*

D1219218

by Gary D. Baldwin

© Copyright 1997

The Glass Press, Inc.
dba Antique Publications
Post Office Box 553 • Marietta, Ohio 45750

PB ISBN# 1-57080-037-5   HB ISBN# 1-57080-038-3

Contents

Foreword

Moser glass is recognized and respected by contemporary glass collectors as representing a unique combination of technical excellence and creative decorative design. Prior to the publication of *Moser—Artistry in Glass* by Gary Baldwin and Lee Carno and *Ludwig Moser, King of Glass* by Mural Charon, the Moser name was associated with only a limited category of decorative styles. With the publication of these reference sources, however, an introduction to the extensive variety of glassware produced by the Moser firm and many of the historical factors which influence Moser production is now available to the general public. *Moser Artistic Glass* is an updated and expanded version of *Moser—Artistry in Glass*. In writing this book it has been the intent of the author to update and clarify information formerly contained in *Moser—Artistry in Glass*, present a new and expanded selection of Moser glassware, consider probable commercial ties which existed between Moser and other glasshouses, provide illustrations of representative Moser look-alike glassware which was produced by rival firms and finally, to include a chapter dealing with the historical and artistic factors which have influenced Moser production after World War II.

Dedication

This book is dedicated to those artists, designers and glass artisans, past and present, who, through an untiring dedication to excellence, have bequeathed to the world the legacy of Central European, and in particular, Moser glass.

Acknowledgments

In grateful recognition of their valuable assistance in making *Moser—Artistry in Glass* as well as the present second edition possible, the author wishes to thank Mrs. Ursula Schubert for her translation and interpretation of what appeared to be an endless series of German articles; personnel at the Corning Museum of Glass, and, in particular, Mrs. Norma Jenkins who was most helpful in the gathering of pertinent information; Mr. Peter Rath of J. & L. Lobmeyr and Dr. Alena Adlerová of the Prague Museum of Decorative Arts for their aid in resolving several controversial issues; and of course the Moser family for providing historical background information heretofore unavailable in the open literature.

Thanks also to contributors to the present edition who include Mr. Tom Pierce of "Tradewinds Furniture & Crystal" (Ellicott City, Maryland) for providing photographs of the circa 1975 Moser glass featured in this book; Mr. and Mrs. Robert Truitt, for many helpful discussions concerning the Bohemian glass industry and for their assistance in obtaining photographs of Bohemian glass contained in Chapter Eight; Dr. Gary Baker, Curator of Glass at the Chrysler Museum of Glass, for graciously providing several important glass photographs; and Mr. Harold Kline (importer of Moser glass) and personnel at the Moser factory for providing photographs of contemporary Moser glassware.

I also wish to express my gratitude to the numerous collectors of Moser glass, both recognized and anonymous, who provided the extensive sampling of glass types recorded here and whose stimulating discussions and observations contributed greatly to my understanding of the subject matter contained within these pages. Finally, but certainly not least, I wish to acknowledge the significant contributions of my spouse without whose understanding, assistance and patience both books would have remained but a noble dream.

Introduction

Published works describing Central European glass production during the latter half of the 19th and first part of the 20th centuries are largely absent from American libraries. Although a considerable number of books and periodicals have been written on this subject, a perceived lack of interest on the part of American collectors has prevented widespread translation of many German texts.

From approximately 1870 to 1938, Central European glasshouses marketed a prodigious variety of luxury glass. Unfortunately, only a small sampling of that output was recorded by contemporary glass historians and many factory records have subsequently been destroyed by the ravages of war. In contrast to the American glass industry which, from a historical and design standpoint, has been reasonably well documented, the intricacies of the Central European glass industry during this period offer an unparalleled opportunity to those interested in the field of investigative journalism.

In writing *Moser—Artistry in Glass* as well as this second edition, the author has organized historical and design information about the Moser firm in such a way as to stimulate, it is hoped, an American renaissance of interest in the fascinating history of Central European glass production. The importance of this knowledge to those interested in American glass cannot be overstated, for it is here that many underlying factors which directly influenced American decorative styles are to be found.

In much the same way that an artist paints on canvas, the term "artistic glass" implies the use of surface decorative techniques such as engraving, cutting or enameling. Pure art glass, on the other hand, relies on glass color, texture and form for its visual appeal. Throughout its history, the Moser firm has exhibited the ability to meld elements of these two artistic concepts into a mutually complementary art form. Based on laurels garnered at multiple international exhibitions, this artistic thrust has, without question, produced some of the highest achievements in the field of decorative glass.

Prior to 1895, Moser artists were acknowledged masters at adapting the themes of romantic painters, as well as Bohemian Renaissance, Baroque, Islamic, Japanese and naturalistic motifs, to create distinctively decorated enameled artware. With the completion of his own glassmaking facilities in 1895, Ludwig Moser's lifelong dream of creating a perfect glass medium to complement his decorative styles was finally realized. Deeply engraved Art Nouveau glass, popular during the 1895–1905 period, was produced by Moser using techniques adopted from Bohemian seal and gem cutters. Created from highly refined shaded blanks colored by newly developed Moser glasses, this artistic style rapidly achieved international recognition. Moser's adaptation of Jan Kotêra's modern concepts in glass cutting and design resulted in an extensive selection of distinctive glassware which is as popular today as when it was first introduced. After World War I, the Moser firm significantly expanded its marketing of enameled glassware.

Although based on traditional decorative themes, this new line of artistic glass exhibited a definite stylistic change from earlier work. Partly as the result of Moser's purchase of Meyr's Neffe's Adolf glassworks in 1922, the enameled glass produced by Moser in the ensuing two decades reached a degree of balance and technical execution unsurpassed in the firm's existence. Perhaps Moser's most important contribution to the world of artistic glass occurred in 1922 when Leo Moser introduced a series of colored rare-earth doped glasses.

Combined with facet cutting techniques designed to emphasize the jewel-like properties of the multicolored glass medium, these new glasses resulted in the Moser firm being awarded top honors at many international exhibitions.

During a relatively short period of 38 years, beginning with the completion of Moser's Meierhöfen works in 1895 and terminating with the total acquisition of the firm by the Bohemian Union Bank in 1933, Moser Glassworks rose to the international pinnacle of success. As a result of the firm's dedication to artistic and technical standards of the highest possible level, the quality of the crystal mass and perfection of cut was unsurpassed by any other contemporary glasshouse. Moser glass became the cherished possession of royalty and other important personages throughout the world and was justifiably referred to as the "Glass of Kings."

Just as in the past, the present-day Moser firm is dedicated to creating artistic glass of the highest possible quality. Contemporary Czech artists, designers and glass artisans are responsible for an ever increasing volume of high quality glassware based on contemporary artistic themes as well as on traditional Moser designs. As a result of these efforts, the contemporary Moser factory is recognized as one of the finest producers of artistic glass in Central Europe.

In writing this book the author has employed available sources to develop a comprehensive historical record of the Moser firm. Considerable information has been obtained from articles published in the *Czech Glass Review*, as well as from German books and records contemporary with the time period of interest. Much of the narrative regarding Ludwig Moser's early years was derived from records brought to this country by Leo Moser and retained by the Corning Museum of Glass. Biographical sketches on Leo and Richard Moser are largely a result of personal interviews with members of the Moser family. Information regarding post-WWII Moser production was derived from a comprehensive brochure on Moser glass produced by Alena Adlerová, PhD.

Moser glass has long been an enigma to many glass collectors. Certainly the Moser name is widely recognized as connotating high quality; however, a full understanding of the broad scope of Moser products remains, even today, somewhat illusive. As an aid to the process of identification we have segregated the majority of Moser glass into generic categories based on prominent decorative features and/or techniques. This approach is generally based on a foundation of signed Moser examples and should prove valuable in the identification of pieces heretofore lacking proper attribution. Illustrated glassware which is designated "Moser" is either signed or has an attribution based on signed examples. Glassware, which in the opinion of the author was marketed by Moser but lacks an irrefutable provenance, is designated as "attributed to Moser." Further aids to identification are provided by a summary of the technical characteristics exhibited by Moser glass, including information regarding glass types, fluorescent properties and construction techniques.

Geographical locations throughout Bohemia have been identified using the names appropriate to the time frame in which they are mentioned. Prior to 1918, many of the prominent Czech glassmaking centers bore German names; after the fall of the Austro-Hungarian Empire, these names were replaced by their former Czech equivalents. A cross-reference of German and Czech geographic nomenclature is provided in the "Town Cross-Reference" section at the back of this book, on page 182.

Historical background and technique development provide necessary ingredients for the full appreciation of fine artistic glass. In the final analysis, however, visual appeal has the last word in establishing the success or failure of a particular design. As one progresses through the following pages, the true magic of Moser dances before your eyes. From the earliest complex and intricate creations to the jewel-like simplicity of the Modern and Art Deco facet-cut styles, one cannot help but be impressed by the consistency of decorative balance and artistic execution. Unquestionably, visual appeal and Moser glass are synonymous terms.

I. Karlsbad's Rise to International Prominence

Bohemia had established itself as a leader in Central European glass production as early as the second half of the 14th century. There is evidence that even in this early period limited amounts of Bohemian glassware was being exported to foreign markets. From these humble beginnings emerged what was perhaps the most extensive network of glass exporting facilities yet recorded. By the latter half of the 17th century, Česká Lípa was recognized as the foremost Bohemian center of glass manufacturing and trade. Engravers and enamelists, operating either as private individuals or out of small shops, decorated glass bought from the major factories. The finished products were then exported or sold at the major centers of commerce located throughout Bohemia.

Continuing success in the export of Bohemian glass was ensured after 1750 by the construction of permanent warehouses in all of the important ports and cities in Europe, as well as overseas. To cultivate foreign markets, advanced sales and display techniques were used to attract wealthy and influential buyers. Special sales rooms were established in important towns, and trade people and the nobility were invited to inspect the displayed glassware. At these locations, demonstrations of engraving and enameling techniques were frequently arranged. Individual artists traveled about the countryside carrying with them the equipment necessary to produce customized decorations such as inscriptions, monograms or coats of arms. In addition, shops were set up in the heavily frequented spa areas for the convenience of wealthy patrons.

Bohemian glass production experienced a rapid growth during the 18th century. In 1753, 58 glassworks are known to have been in operation; by 1799, this total increased to 79 with approximately 3,000 people being employed. Records show that 8,209 metric tons of glass were exported to foreign markets in 1805; by 1825, this number had increased to 23,780 metric tons. During this period the traditional customers of Bohemia were Turkey, Spain, Portugal, the German states and Northern Italy. In 1855, 83 glasshouses were active in Bohemia. These houses produced three-fifths of all the glass manufactured in the Austrian state, and employed some 120,000 workers. Principal manufacturers were Harrach in Neuwelt (Nový Svêt) and Meyr's Neffe[1] in Winterberg (Vimperk) and Eleonorenhain (Lenora). Luxury glass produced by these firms was primarily exported to England, Germany, Switzerland and Italy. Karlsbad (Karlovy Vary), a renowned spa dating from the 17th century and presently capital of the Czech Republic's Karlovy Vary province, is situated 1,225 feet above sea level at the intersection of the Tepel and Eger rivers. As illustrated in an early view by the artist L. Buquoy, Karlsbad appears to cling to the foothills of the precipitous Erzgebirge mountain range as it rises tier upon tier above the valley floor. Known chiefly for the curative properties of no fewer than 17 warm springs, Karlsbad attracted nobility and wealthy patrons from all over the world.

These springs, ranging in temperature from 108° to 164° F and believed to originate from a common reservoir, are free from any color or odor and are consequently used for drinking and bathing. The chemical composition of the spring water is considered valuable in the treatment of liver diseases and other ailments produced by uric acid. Spa waters were considered sufficiently potent that special medical and treatment centers were established to properly administer their medicinal properties.

Spa waters were first used for bathing in 1520, but the rapid growth of the town as an international health resort dates from the middle of the 19th century. Much of this success was the responsibility of the renowned physician Jean de Carro (1770–1857), whose tireless efforts as a champion of the adoption of vaccination brought him worldwide acclaim. From the time de Carro settled in Karlsbad in 1826, his intensive cultural, organizational and scientific activities permeated all aspects of Karlsbad's social life.

In an effort to infuse the latest scientific developments into the thinking of the spa's physicians, de Carro extensively studied contemporary therapeutic procedures and, as a result, published several books dealing with new and modern methods of spa treatment. These books, translated into several languages, found worldwide acceptance and brought a flood of patrons from as far away as the Near East, India and the United States. In addition to his scientific endeavors, de Carro initiated reforms among the hotel and boarding house proprietors

---

[1]Spelling appears as "Meyr's Neffe" on the factory letterhead; in the Moser factory records, the form "Meyer's Neffe" is used.

to improve guest accommodations. He also became deeply involved in the spa's cultural activities. History, literature, music and art formed a common basis upon which many long-lasting and influential acquaintances were established. To further publicize spa activities, de Carro annually published (in French) the *Karlsbad Almanac* which provided information about upcoming events for the spa season. Jean de Carro's almost superhuman efforts to transform Karlsbad into the foremost European spa resort were only terminated by his death on March 12, 1857.

At the same time that Karlsbad was developing as a spa, its porcelain and stoneware industries were becoming prominent. Production of luxury porcelain and stoneware items was supported by the existence of local supplies of high grade kaolin and ornamental stone; coal was readily available from the Falkenau basin, located several kilometers west of Karlsbad. During the off-season, Karlsbad was a typical mid-19th century industrial town. In June and July, when the spa season was at its height, Karlsbad assumed a façade consistent with the presence of wealth and nobility.

Glass cutters and engravers began settling in Karlsbad during the first half of the 18th century. Of these men, only the name Bartholomew Teller has been recorded. In this early period, artistic endeavors rarely exceeded the decoration of spa drinking cups. Somewhat later, J. M. Tellner and his son J. O. Tellner rose to prominence. J. O. Tellner is credited with the actual founding of the Karlsbad engraving and cutting craft and was the teacher of the most famous of all Karlsbad engravers, Andreas Vincenz Peter Mattoni (signed articles bear the signature "A. H. Mattoni").

Mattoni (1779–1864), a native of Karlsbad, was recognized by contemporaries as an exceptionally talented engraver, painter, designer and teacher. Goethe, for example, was numbered among his many customers and admirers. Numerous engraved and decorated cups, beakers and vases, designed and executed by Mattoni, presently exist; several are on display in the Karlovy Vary Museum. In addition to his artistic output, there was a rather large group of glass decorators whose professional genealogy can be traced to the tutorial expertise of this unique individual.[2]

Perhaps the most outstanding of Mattoni's pupils was Anton Pfeiffer (1801–1866). It is said that Pfeiffer's artistic standards surpassed even those of his teacher. Pfeiffer successfully established a workshop in Karlsbad which employed 15 engravers, five glass blowers and five glass painters. Its major emphasis was placed on religious as well as popular spa themes. After his death, Pfeiffer's two brothers, Josef and Jan, carried on in the family tradition. Among Mattoni's other pupils were Rudolf Hiller (1827–1915), who was the first to open a promotional glass showroom in Karlsbad in 1853, and Anton Rudolf Dewitte (1824–1900), a noted engraver of hunting motifs who used decorative styles based on the work of Jakob Gauermann (1773–1845).

Cast before this impressive array of wealth, influence and artistic accomplishments, the birth of Ludwig Moser (1833–1916) heralded the rise of Karlsbad to even greater heights. Born in Karlsbad on June 18, 1833, Ludwig was the son of a tailor by the name of Lazar Moser and his wife Henretta née Becherová. Lazar and his wife settled in Karlsbad and shortly after, in 1820, Lazar was the first Jew in Karlsbad to be granted trade and traveling papers. After attending elementary school in Karlsbad, Ludwig Moser completed four years of high school taught by the Pearists (a Catholic monastic order) in Vienna; he returned to Karlsbad in 1847 to finish his high school education. In 1847 he became an engraving apprentice to Andreas Mattoni while simultaneously taking painting classes from the painter Ernst Anton; this phase of his education continued until 1850.

According to Ludwig Moser's travel log, a type of travel passport issued on October 9, 1850 (this log was retained by the Moser family but was lost during the Nazi takeover in 1938), family financial considerations forced Ludwig to seek work outside of Karlsbad. Ludwig traveled by foot to Prague in October of 1850, but was unable to acquire a satisfactory position. He continued on to the Grossmann Glass Cutting Company in Polish Kirchen, but there also no employment as an engraver was to be found. Disappointed, Ludwig returned to Prague. In December of 1850, he retraced his steps to Karlsbad where he again served as an apprentice to Mattoni.

After a short period Ludwig again traveled to Prague, this time to study painting under the supervision of the director of the Prague Art Academy, Christian Ruben. To support his studies, Ludwig worked as an engraver at the Wilhelm Hoffman Glass Company, "Am

---

[2]Anton Urban(1845–1909) was a pupil of Anton Pfeiffer; his elder brother, Joseph Urban (died 1895), was a pupil of Mattoni. Anton Urban taught Jundrich Pfeiffer (born 1866) who was the last of the family line. Both Urban brothers are noted for their engraved spa themes, coats of arms and hunting motifs. Their descendants continued the art of engraving into the 20th century with Julius Urban (born 1883) being the last independent engraver in Karlsbad. Jindrich Boltz and Eduard Low are also recorded as being pupils of Mattoni.

Fig. 1 Disassembled amethyst and clear Bohemian crystal Zwischengoldglas tumbler. Attributed to Ludwig Moser by the Moser family, c. 1865–70. Height 3³/₄". Collection of Mr. and Mrs. Harry Foreman.

Graben" ("On the Ditch"), for a Herr Eberl. In 1853 he returned to Karlsbad to work for the glass engraver Anton Pfeiffer, but low pay and pressing family responsibilities forced him to travel to Germany in 1854 in search of a better position. Ludwig traveled from Zwickau to Leipzig, without success, and thence on to Berlin where he found work in an engraving shop in the Markgrafenstrasse (Land Dukes Street). During his seven month stay in Berlin, Ludwig joined the workers' union and gained considerable recognition as an engraver of hunting and ornamental motifs.

Upon his return to Karlsbad from Berlin in 1855, Ludwig rented a "boutique" from Mattoni on the "Alten Wiesen" ("Old Meadow") near the Hotel Pupp. During the summer months, he engraved monograms, writings, seals and ornaments on drinking cups and other glass items and, on occasion, on semiprecious stones. When the spa season was over, he worked for his parents at their home in the house "Zwei Prinzen" ("Two Princes"). In the latter part of the 1850s, Ludwig married a local Karlsbad girl. Of the six children born to the couple, only the sons Rudolf (1860–1908), Friedrich (born 1863) and Oskar (born 1864) lived long enough to become involved in the evolution of the glassworks founded by their father.

Although Ludwig Moser studied painting and engraving and was known as an accomplished artist in his own right, the world-renowned legacy of this man was not related to his artistic works, but rather to the founding and direction of a glass manufacturing firm dedicated to the perfection of artistic glass. Well aware of Jean de Carro's former successes, Ludwig also possessed exceptional organizational abilities and a keen commercial sense. He was, without question, an entrepreneur of the first rank. At the age of 24 years (1857), Ludwig cast aside the trappings of an isolated engraving studio and, in the manner of Rudolf Hiller and A. H. Pfeiffer, embarked on the establishment of a series of glass showrooms supported by a highly talented staff of designers, enamelists and engravers.

II. Ludwig Moser (1857–1893)
Glass Decorator and Entrepreneur

In March of 1857 Ludwig Moser paid 65 guilden for a former restaurant which he converted into a well-equipped engraving studio. This studio was located in the Marktbrunnen Strasse (Market Fountain Street) near the sanatorium promenade in Karlsbad. Ludwig was subsequently granted a license to decorate and sell glass products in the local area. Within a relatively short period of time, the growing demand for his engravings and stone cuttings resulted in the opening of several new shops within the immediate vicinity. In spite of these early successes, 36 years would pass before Ludwig would be granted the right to melt his own glass. During those years, Moser hired talented artists from the regions surrounding Karlsbad and Steinschönau (Kamenický Šenov) in northern Bohemia.

In the process, he created a progressive and commercially successful business which attracted the patronage of royal houses throughout Europe. In addition, his merchandising acumen led to the development of a worldwide trade network which, in combination with unique products of the highest possible quality, brought him international recognition.

Commercial success in glass merchandising depends largely on establishing clientele with artistic appreciation as well as the financial means to purchase the goods offered. With this in mind, Ludwig opened multiple commercial outlets in the most socially influential sections of Karlsbad. Moser's first retail shop was located in the spa institution known as "Umesta Výmura" ("By the Town of Weimer"). He opened a second shop in 1862 in the spa institution "Uzlatého Klíče" ("The Golden Key") and, in 1865, a third shop in the house known as "U červeného srdce" ("The Red Heart"). The latter shop offered the most elaborate salesroom in Karlsbad and was strategically located on the main street (known as the "Old Meadow") of the spa quarter. For his own paintings and designs, Moser purchased raw glass from the best south Bohemian glass blowing companies Meyr's Neffe (in Winterberg), Wilhelm Kralik (in Eleonorenhain) and Löetz Witwe (in Klostermühle). Light fixtures to be decorated were purchased from Pallme at Steinschönau. During this period the ranks of the fledgling Moser firm swelled to encompass several dozen local workers.

In 1860, cut products marketed by Moser gained favorable recognition at the Industrial Exhibition in Vienna. In 1862, Moser won a medal at the World Exhibition in London. In response to the increased product demand which accompanied these accolades, Ludwig Moser opened a new decorating workshop at Meistersdorf[1] (Mistrovice) near Steinschönau. This facility, organized around 1870, included engraving and cutting shops and a large enameling studio under the direction of a Herr Kneipe. From its inception, the Moser firm employed only the finest engravers, cutters and enamelists. With the opening of the Meistersdorf facility,

Fig. 2 Spa cups were available to Spa clientele in a wide variety of shapes and decorative motifs.

these highly skilled artists and artisans were primarily recruited from the north Bohemian region of Haida (Nový Bor) and Steinschönau.

As might be expected, many of the artistic styles indigenous to this area of Bohemia were strongly reflected in the glassware marketed by the Moser firm during the 1870–1893 period. Sparse records have yielded the names of only a few of the most prominent

---

[1]Meistersdorf was known as the "Village of Masters" and was the source of many of the finest artists and engravers to emerge from Bohemia (ref. Alfred S. Johnston, *The Fritsche Ewer*, New York, 1886).

designers/engravers who worked for the Moser firm during this early period. Names of enamelists are strangely absent from printed records. Among Moser's employees were Eduard Hoffman (died 1878) and his son Johann (1842–1900). These men were exceptionally talented engravers who specialized in figural motifs. In addition to the example in Figure 3, further references to the work of Johann Hoffman may be found in Corning's *Czechoslovakian Glass and Glas des Historismus* by

Fig. 3 Engraved covered goblet entitled "Gretchen Accompanied by Faust." Executed by Johann F. Hoffman, Karlsbad, after 1882. Unsigned. Collection of the Prague Museum of Decorative Arts (inventory no. 74465).

Walter Spiegl. It is recorded that Ludwig Lobmeyr (then acting director of the Viennese based glasshouse of J. & L. Lobmeyr), upon observation of the engraved glass sent by Johann Hoffman to the 1873 Vienna Exhibition, commented that although Hoffman's work did not always adhere to accepted compositional guidelines, his engraving technique satisfied the highest expectations.

Emanuel Hoffman, a portrait engraver of considerable importance, and his son Jan worked for Moser for many years. Additional names include Joseph Urban and Rudolf Hiller, both of whom were students of Andreas Mattoni; their respective sons; and the artists/engravers Sacher, Dietl and Nowak (known for his figurals and ornamental decorations). At the 1873 Vienna World Exhibition, Moser's display featured large cups engraved with figural scenes by Johann Hoffman based on popular paintings by Wilhelm van Kaulback (1805–1874) and Friedrich Gauermann (1807–1862).

Due to their geographical proximity, a portion of the raw glass consumed by the Meistersdorf branch was purchased from factories around Haida and Steinschönau; Emanuel Hoffman is said to have obtained most of his glass blanks from Graff Harrach (Nový Svêt). Meyr's Neffe in Winterberg (Vimperk) has been singled out as a principal supplier of glass to the Meistersdorf facility.

By 1873, Moser was managing five individual shops, the Meistersdorf refinery (which employed some 56 workers) and sales outlets in St. Petersburg, New York, Paris and London. In that same year, the glass shop, cutting and engraving workshops, and the inventory of the Imperial and Royal Privileged "Burgstein" Mirror Factory at Röhrsdorf (Sloup) came under his control. After 1874, Moser's expansion and commercial thrusts were overshadowed by his desire to obtain permission to build his own glassworks in the Karlsbad area. Nearly 20 frustrating years were spent fighting the corrupt and anti-Semitic Austrian bureaucracy before his dream was finally realized.

Initially, Moser merchandised not only his own glass products but also those of other glass decorators in the Karlsbad area. As Moser's dominance in the marketplace increased, however, many of these decorators probably found it necessary to merge with the Moser firm to secure a continuing outlet for their artistic endeavors. Advertisements from the period attest to the wide assortment of glassware sold. Included were mirrors and a large selection of tableware in fine Muslin glass and in cut crystal.[2]

Moser's products often featured traditional engraved or gilded monograms and emblems, or engraved hunting scenes. More intricate and artistically challenging compositions were also offered. Of primary importance to the identification of glassware produced during this period, was the consensus by contemporary experts that engraved glass marketed by Moser in the Karlsbad region exhibited artistic characteristics which were unique.

This attribution was the result of Moser's use of themes generated by contemporary painters as well as free interpretation of Czech Renaissance and Baroque glass forms. Consequently, one can conclude that the majority of Moser engraved glass did not have counterparts produced by other Central European glasshouses during this early period.

Ludwig Moser ranks as a pioneer of the modern glass industry which began to develop in Bohemia in the middle of the 19th century. During this period, the Bohemian glass industry, based on the ever improving technology associated with the Industrial Revolution, as well as on progressive management and marketing techniques, was developing the ability to succeed in the highly competitive international trade arena.

Artistic ideas originating in England also began to influence Bohemia. These ideas were concerned with the function of art and the manner in which it could be used to enhance human environments. Moser used these concepts, but in reverse he created environments which would enhance the value of the artistic glass he sold. Moser's salesrooms were effective not only from an aesthetic standpoint, but also from a commercial one. They represented an early embodiment of the idea that artistically fine items placed in the correct environment will sell themselves.

In addition to selling in shops during the relatively short-lived spa season, Moser became heavily involved in exhibitions and artistic auctions. A letter preserved in the Karlovy Vary Museum, written to Moser by the director of the Museum of Art and Industry in Vienna and dated January 14, 1869 states:

> "Mr. Ludwig Moser, industrial glassmaker of Karlsbad, has several times exhibited articles of crystal glass in this museum which where outstanding for their technical perfection of cut."

At the 1873 Vienna World Exhibition, the exhibits which featured the work of Johann Hoffman resulted in Moser's being awarded a Medal for Merits. As a result of subsequent sales, Moser shortly thereafter acquired the enviable distinction of being appointed supplier of glass to the Austrian Imperial Court of Franz Joseph.

Moser also exhibited at the 1878 Paris International Exposition where he introduced enameled and gilded glass imitating Islamic goldsmiths' work and Japanese floral motifs. These patented designs were acquired from the Ceramic Art School at Teplice and, in different variants, remained in the inventory of the glassworks for several decades. A noted contemporary French art critic, who was known to comment favorably only on French art, complimented Moser's efforts to effect a significant change in Bohemian artistic glass styles. It is recorded in an advertisement in *A Guide to Karlsbad*, published in 1880 and written by Dr. E. Hlaváĉek, that Moser products had received many honorable prizes at various exhibitions. Specific information regarding the dates and locations of many of these exhibitions has not been documented; however, there is little doubt that Moser was rapidly becoming one of the foremost artistic glass suppliers in Central Europe. The growing influence of the Moser firm is reflected in the appointment of Ludwig Moser as a member of the jury (in this context, juries were responsible for judging glass competitions) for the Austro-Hungarian Confederation at the 1889 World Exhibition in Paris. Participation in shows in Glasgow and Edinburgh resulted in Moser's appointment to the glass jury for these areas.

In contrast to the laurels being garnered in Europe, Moser's marketing efforts in New York were apparently beset by numerous difficulties. As recorded in an 1887 trade journal, excessive appraisals by customs agents, low product demand, and high costs associated with maintaining a New York showroom forced the sales representative, Rudolph Moser, to terminate operations. In 1891, a new outlet was established by Rudolf's brother Oskar at No. 23 Union Square. After five years of operation, this shop was forced to close, with all remaining stock being turned over for public auction.

After the death of his first wife, Ludwig married Julie Meyer (of the Meyer glassmaking family) around 1875. This union was blessed by the birth of four sons: Carl, Gustov, Leo (1879–1974) and Richard. Carl Moser was educated as a doctor and did not become involved in the glassmaking industry. Gustov later moved to Paris

---

[2]Muslin glass: In the early days, Muslin glass was produced by overlaying glass with wax-soaked lace material and submerging the combination in an acid bath. The resulting pattern had the appearance of fine muslin cloth.

Fig. 4 *Left to right:* Gustov, Leo, Richard and Carl Moser.

where, for many years, he managed the Moser factory outlet on the Boulevard des Italiens. From the early 20th century on, Leo and Richard served the Moser firm in various capacities, finally becoming the firm's artistic and commercial directors, respectively.

A major flood in the late fall of 1891 caused extensive damage to the residential, resort and commercial areas of Karlsbad. Out of this devastation grew a new and modernized city and for Ludwig Moser, a larger display room in the "Roten Herz." Increased sales, persistent difficulties associated with acquiring suitable raw glass, and the extreme distance to the Meistersdorf refinery (85–100 miles) brought about a renewed effort to obtain approval to construct a modern glass manufacturing company and refinery in the town of Meierhöfen, only three kilometers from Karlsbad.[3] On June 4, 1892, the Ministry of the Interior in Vienna finally granted the Moser firm permission to build glass furnaces in the Karlsbad area.

The years 1857–1893 represent a period in Moser history about which little has been written. Much of the information contained in this chapter, particularly with respect to Moser's Meistersdorf facility, was derived from records brought to this country by Leo Moser and retained by the Corning Museum of Glass.

---

[3]In Central European terminology, a glass refinery is responsible for the decoration of glass, not the melting and forming of glass blanks.

III. Meierhöfen (1893–1938)
Ludwig Moser's Dream Fulfilled

The year 1893 marked the opening of Ludwig Moser's new glasshouse at Meierhöfen. This facility, organized as a joint stock company by Ludwig Moser and his three elder sons, Rudolf, Oskar and Friedrich under the name "Karlsbader Glasindustrie Gesellschaft Ludwig Moser & Söhne, A. G. Meierhöfen bei Karlsbad," not only represented the long-awaited fulfillment of Moser's dreams, but also the foundation for one of the most technically innovative and artistically precise sources of fine glass the world has ever known.

The entire management of the Moser firm was moved to Meierhöfen, and the new facility was staffed with the foremost glassmakers and cutters available in Bohemia. These glass artisans, partially attracted by the offer of free modern housing and heating, were primarily recruited from the Sumava mountain region in southern Bohemia. Richard Kralik was appointed works foreman and chief melter; Rudolf Novak became foreman of the cutting workshop.[1] Both of these men came from Meyr's Neffe's Adolf glassworks at Winterberg and were renowned for their expertise in the production of high quality Bohemian crystal. Attached to the main glass factory was an extensive glass decorating studio which employed the region's finest artists and designers. At this point in time, the Moser Glassworks consisted of 350 employees.

An interesting postscript to the opening of the Meierhöfen works is provided by the testimony of a retired glass blower who worked for the Moser firm for over 30 years. According to his account, recorded in the March 1960 issue of the East German periodical *Weltbuehne*, 1895 was the earliest date at which the glass-melting furnaces became operational. At that time the first in a series of financial crises hit the Moser firm. In his preoccupation with constructing a glassworks of uncompromising capability, Ludwig Moser had simply run out of money. Ludwig called his workers together, apprised them of the situation, and entreated them to remain until business improved. This the workers agreed to do, despite the fact that there was apparently a considerable delay before they once again received compensation for their efforts.

An important type of glass, which contained a large proportion of chalk (calcium carbonate) in combination with potash (potassium carbonate), was first produced in Bohemia about 1680. Because of improved clarity

Fig. 5 Moser factory at Meierhöfen.

---

[1]Richard Kralik (born 1852) was the son of Wilhelm Kralik and Louise Lobmeyr and was a noted poet, musician, philosopher and historian.

Fig. 6 Leo Moser seated in his office at the Meierhöfen glassworks.

and hard brilliance when cut, this new glass, alternately referred to as "chalk glass" or "Bohemian crystal," formed the basis upon which the early Bohemian cut and engraved glass industry flourished.

Although chalk glass represented a significant advancement over the prior glassmaking art, it did not possess the refractive properties and high level of transparency characteristic of the lead crystal developed by Ravenscrift in England. It was also more difficult to shape than lead crystal since it solidified more rapidly when being worked. Through the years, numerous attempts were made to develop a glass which would combine the desirable properties of lead crystal with the rock crystal-like characteristics of chalk glass. One of the most successful of these endeavors was a soda (sodium hydroxide) potash glass manufactured by the Meyr's Neffe's Adolf glassworks. Derivatives of this glass formulation were used throughout Bohemia and Silesia during the second half of the 19th century.

As a testimony to the quality and commercial acceptance of Bohemian crystal, Leo Moser, in an article titled "Commercial Art Glass," which appeared in the March 1942 issue of *The Glass Industry*, stated that "No lead crystal had been produced in Central Europe prior to 1914; all lead crystal had been imported into Central Europe from the U.S., England, France and Belgium." Moser goes on to state that after 1919, Bohemian production of lead crystal increased to the point of reducing imported quantities to the near-zero level. Although, according to the factory melt journal, Moser produced limited amounts of lead crystal after 1919, various forms

of Bohemian crystal have dominated production even up to the present day.

In addition to traditional clear Bohemian crystal, the Moser firm introduced a series of unique new glasses with deep rich colorations. These new colors, introduced after 1895, initially added a distinctive ingredient to engraved Art Nouveau glass which found wide acceptance throughout Europe. In the long term, however, their introduction represented the scientifically innovative foundation upon which the majority of artistic glass produced at Meierhöfen was based.

Concurrent with the firing of the glass furnaces at Meierhöfen came the search for perfection in the manufactured quality of glass. Samples which were judged inferior by Moser's shop supervisors were destroyed. Quality control of this severity, similar to that practiced at the Steuben Glass Works, resulted in a well-deserved reputation for producing flawless glassware equal to the best produced by any contemporary manufacturer. Deeply engraved Art Nouveau and Modern style glassware are just two of many examples which bear witness to the success of this philosophy.

Even before the advent of World War I, examples of Moser glass were among the most valued possessions of world rulers, wealthy personages, statesmen and diplomats. Mass production techniques have never been employed at the Moser Glassworks. Even though multiple copies of popular glass items have been produced, each example represents an original and unique artistic achievement.

Initially, glass products marketed by the Moser firm included wine sets, tableware, vases, bowls, jardinieres, jewel and ashtrays, spa cups and other decorative glass. Most of these items could be obtained as unadorned crystal, engraved and/or gilded, or with enameled embellishments. As it was prior to 1893, custom work for important clientele remained a growing and ever important segment of Moser production. With the passage of time, the selection of shapes and decorative styles was constantly expanded. Many decorative forms, which had their designs firmly rooted in 19th century neo-Renaissance and neo-Baroque styles, were also produced during the first quarter of the 20th century. Some popular items, such as Art Nouveau tableware in the "Paolo" (factory designation; named after Leo Moser's wife) or "Rose" pattern (Plate 125), remained in continuous production and is presently available from the Moser factory.

The composition of drinking and table sets grew to encompass new types of stemware and tumblers designed specifically for various wines, liqueurs and cognacs; slender champagne goblets; beer tankards; glasses for water and other beverages; finger bowls; fruit and sweetmeat bowls; jugs and decanters. In consort with this exceptional selection of tableware was the world famous Moser banquet table set which has become the cherished possession of world rulers and other important people; these sets typically bore engraved monograms or other decorations highlighted with 24K gold.

After the Moser firm recovered from its initial financial difficulties, its business opportunities increased at a heady pace. Due in part to sponsored shows, ranging from Cairo to Bombay to New York, Ludwig Moser recognized that a worldwide network of commercial outlets was required to ensure the sale of his company's products. The Brussels World Exhibition in 1897, at which Ludwig was vice president of the glass jury, proved financially quite successful for the firm. In the summer of 1897, Ludwig decided to establish a new shop in Paris. It opened in October of that year under the management of his son Gustov. Located in the "Maison Doree" on the Boulevard des Italiens, Moser's Paris out-

Fig. 8 "Copenhagen" table service, cut and decorated with high-relief gold (prod. no. 99000). Designed about 1910, produced up to the present. Moser factory photograph.

Fig. 7 "Splendid" table service, cut and decorated with high-relief gold (prod. no. 10160). Designed after 1910, produced up to the present. Moser factory photograph; collection of Tradewinds Furniture & Crystal.

Fig. 9 "Copenhagen" water pitcher. Height 11⅞". Collection of Tradewinds Furniture & Crystal.

let exists to the present day. A steady increase in the volume of spa clientele, as well as a highly acclaimed participation in the 1900 World Exhibition in Paris, skyrocketed the name of Moser glass into international prominence.

An insight into the production capability of the Moser firm during this period is provided by a listing of facilities in the Austria-Hungary Glass Industry index for the year 1910. The Meierhöfen plant is recorded as having two melting ovens with 20 open ports (four with caps) fired by a brown-coal Siebert system; 88 steam-driven cutting workbenches; and painting, engraving, etching and printing departments. A total of 400 employees produced a yearly output of 6,000 metric tons. Workers in front of the ovens typically labored under what were termed "Austrian patriotic conditions": 12-hour shifts and no vacation or insurance benefits.

As a good businessman, Moser knew that appreciation of fine glass is rarely spontaneous but that, rather, it grows with an exposure to the whole artistic and technical process of glassmaking. With this in mind, the Moser firm allowed clients to witness the making of glass from "working of the melt" to the finished product in on-site

Fig. 10 "Royal" table service, cut (prod. no. 9000). Designed about 1908, produced up to the present. Moser factory photograph.

sales rooms (this technique is still being employed by the Steuben Glass Works in Corning, New York). Personalities so honored included King Edward VII of England, the Shah of Persia, the King of Siam, and the Maharajahs of Hyderabad and Travancore. Edward VII was sufficiently impressed with the quality of Moser glass that he ordered a complete set of tableware, now known as the "Royal" set.

This set was later duplicated for Edward's wife, Queen Alexandra, and for King Haakon VII of Norway and Turkish Sultan Abdul Hamid. According to a 1964 article in the *Czech Glass Review*, the "Royal" set, in a somewhat modernized version, was still being used on official occasions by all contemporary Czechoslovakian embassies and diplomatic missions. Moser also organized a tour service which, in cooperation with the hotel and spa institutions located in Karlsbad, was designed to alleviate the boredom of wealthy potential clientele. These tours, with a stop in luxurious sample rooms from which articles could be purchased, succeeded in introducing the world of glassmaking to an otherwise disinterested segment of society.

The Moser firm's further expansion at home and abroad was initiated by the opening in 1903 of a sales outlet in the house known as "Berliner Hof" on Kaiserstrasse in Marienbad (Mariánské Láznê). Initially, this sales outlet was managed by Richard Moser. In 1905, sales outlets were realized in the Palace Hotel in Franzensbad (Františkovy Láznê) and the "Galleria Vittorio Emmanuele" in Milano. An additional shop was opened in Teplitz and, finally, a large and important sales outlet was established in Prague. Foreign sales were supported by branch offices, such as on the Boulevard des Italiens in Paris and in Bombay, India, which were staffed either by members of the Moser family or by other experienced personnel.

A factory training program was instituted by the Moser firm to develop sales personnel with expertise in the closely related fields of artistic glass and porcelain. These people were responsible for placing Moser products in independently owned shops in the spa areas and in stores throughout the world known to specialize in quality artistic items.

One is inclined to stop and speculate on the reason for training sales personnel to be experts in the dual fields of glass and porcelain. As early as 1870 Ludwig Moser had established strong commercial and artistic ties with the Teplitz Ceramic Art School. This relationship dealt primarily with design development and, interestingly enough, is probably responsible for the

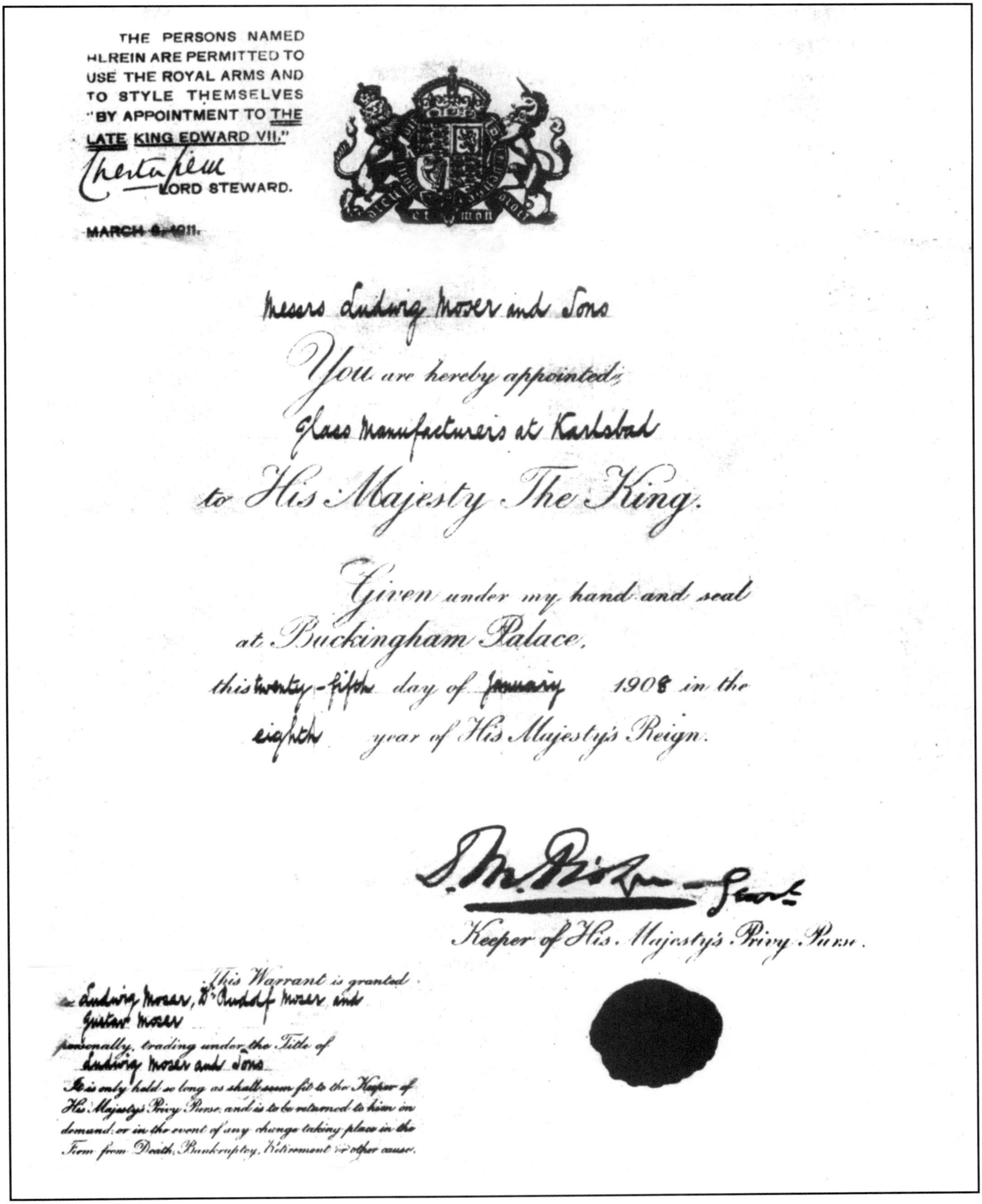

THE PERSONS NAMED
HEREIN ARE PERMITTED TO
USE THE ROYAL ARMS AND
TO STYLE THEMSELVES
"BY APPOINTMENT TO THE
LATE KING EDWARD VII."

Thertafell
LORD STEWARD.

MARCH 6, 1911.

Messrs Ludwig Moser and Sons

You are hereby appointed;

Glass manufacturers at Karlsbad

to His Majesty The King.

Given under my hand and seal

at Buckingham Palace,

this twenty-fifth day of January 1908 in the

eighth year of His Majesty's Reign.

S. M. Bishop
Keeper of His Majesty's Privy Purse.

This Warrant is granted
to Ludwig Moser, Dr Rudolf Moser and
Gustav Moser
personally, trading under the Title of
Ludwig Moser and Sons
It is only held so long as shall seem fit to the Keeper of
His Majesty's Privy Purse, and is to be returned to him on
demand, or in the event of any change taking place in the
Firm from Death, Bankruptcy, Retirement or other cause.

Fig. 11 Document of appointment as supplier of glass to the English Court of Edward VII.

similarity between Moser glass and Teplitz porcelain decorative patterns which is occasionally encountered.

Karlsbad and its environs were noted for the production of fine quality porcelain and these products were undoubtedly marketed by Ludwig Moser during the formative years of his firm. In particular, the Epiag china factory in Karlsbad, which was owned and managed by another branch of the Moser family, produced high quality porcelain products well into the 1930s. Due to the extensive differences in the manufacturing techniques required to produce and decorate glass and porcelain, it is highly unlikely that the Moser glass factory would have directly engaged in the processing of porcelain products. Considering the extensive network of worldwide outlets established by Ludwig Moser, however, it does seem probable that the Moser firm marketed the porcelain products of selected manufacturers as an adjunct to their own output of artistic glass.

As indicated by the listing at the end of this chapter, participation in international shows continued with an important showing at the World Exhibition in St.-Louis in 1904. On January 25, 1908, the Moser firm was appointed "Glass Manufacturers at Karlsbad" to his Majesty Edward VII of England; this prestigious title was renewed after the King's death in 1911. Moser's penetration of world markets in combination with an unwavering dedication to excellence had earned for his glass the enviable title of the "Glass of Kings."

A reorganization of the Moser firm, occurring around 1900, left Rudolf Moser as the acting director. About this time, specific references regarding Ludwig Moser disappear from the available literature. One suspects that Ludwig, by then 67, preferred to turn over a major portion of the company management to his younger and more energetic sons. Considering his intimate involvement with glassmaking, Ludwig most likely remained in the background in the capacity of controlling interest and technical consultant until his death on September 27, 1916. Evidence suggests that when Rudolf died in 1908, Leo Moser assumed the duties of commercial director for a short period of time. In 1916, Richard Moser became the commercial director and Leo, the artistic director.

As World War I began in the summer of 1914, Moser production was dramatically reduced. Loss of spa clientele, the drafting of many into the military, the severance of commercial ties to related industries and the loss of lucrative foreign markets were responsible for this decline. An extremely important characteristic of a hand-processed industry is its ability to adapt to rapidly changing artistic styles or market requirements with a minimum loss of time and money. At no other point in history was this ability more important to the survival of the Moser firm. Under the direction of Leo Moser, product lines previously designed to fit the specialized requirements of various side branches were modified to be compatible with whatever export or internal markets could be uncovered. As an example, in 1916 Moser introduced a series of cups which imitated in the finest detail the glasses produced originally by Johann Mildner (1763–1808). These cups were enameled with a miniature portrait of Emperor Wilhelm II and bore the inscription "Gott mit uns, Wilhelm"; they apparently made excellent gifts in patriotic circles. This hand-to-mouth existence proved successful, and by the spring of 1916 business began a slow upward turn.

With the capitulation of Austria-Hungary on October 28, 1918, Czechoslovakia was declared an independent state by the national committee in Prague. Karlsbad and Meierhöfen, once part of the rich and powerful Austro-Hungarian Empire, found themselves within the boundaries of this newly formed Czechoslovakian state. Although names and national boundaries were changed (Karlsbad assumed its original name of Karlovy Vary and Meierhöfen was renamed Dvory), the high quality of Moser glass remained unaltered. In fact, glass produced by the Moser firm during the following decade would reach a pinnacle of perfection and worldwide recognition unrivaled throughout the prior years of the firm's existence.

Immediately following the cessation of hostilities, the market for artistic glass increased perceptibly. Although this proved to be but a brief respite before the gathering storm, it apparently instilled sufficient confidence in Richard Moser to enter into negotiations for the acquisition of several rival firms. When the value of the Kronen finally collapsed in the wake of World War I, these negotiations were terminated, and Richard was forced to seek aid from the Bohemian Union Bank to forestall imminent bankruptcy. Controlling interest in the Moser firm was acquired by the Union Bank who assumed full financial responsibility; Richard and Leo were retained on the board of directors. Even though the management of Ludwig Moser and Söhne had now passed irretrievably out of family hands, Leo Moser, as artistic director, continued to exert a dramatic influence over the firm's output of artistic glass. Richard Moser, being largely relieved of the financial burdens normally associated with his post as commercial director, was free to cultivate the friendship of influential people and expand the visibility of the Moser firm through its representation at important international expositions.

In 1922, the Moser firm merged with the Meyr's Neffe's Adolf glassworks at Winterberg (Vimperk) to form a limited company by the rather lengthy name of "The Karlsbad Factory for Crystal Glass Ltd. Co. Ludwig Moser and Sons and Meyer's Nephews."[2]

With the acquisition of the Adolf works, the total Moser plant was increased to include six glass ovens with 68 ports, 248 cutting workbenches, an additional engraving and painting department, and 750 workers. According to the 1925 edition of the *Address Book of the European Glass Industry* (published by the magazine *The Glass Huette*) a Herr Benno Hess was named acting director of the Adolf works. The merger of Moser Glassworks with Meyr's Neffe not only dramatically increased the firm's capacity for producing artistic glass, but considerably increased the firm's access to the cumulative design capacity of leading Viennese artists. Artistic glass designed by Otto Prutscher, Professor Josef Hoffman of the School of Applied Art in Vienna, and the Wiener Werkstätte association of artists was incorporated into Moser's product lines.

In light of the significant artistic influence which the Wiener Werkstätte was destined to exert on Moser production, it would seem appropriate to digress a few moments and present a historical synopsis of this internationally acclaimed design organization.

In response to the freedom of the Art Nouveau movement sweeping Europe, a group of Viennese painters, sculptors and architects formed an association known as the Vienna Secession in 1897. Koloman Moser (1868–1918) and Josef Olbrich (1867–1908), charter members of the Vienna Secession, were commissioned by E. Bakalowitz Söhn of Vienna to design decorative vases and tableware; these designs, in turn, were produced by several Bohemian glasshouses, including Meyr's Neffe.[3]

In 1900, Koloman Moser and Josef Hoffman (1870–1956) organized the Eighth Secession (Art Nouveau) Exhibition to which, among others, had been invited Charles Rennie Mackintosh, his wife Margaret Macdonald, and Charles Robert Ashbee and his Guild of Handicrafts. On a subsequent visit to Scotland and London, Moser was sufficiently impressed with the workshop system developed by Ashbee that he returned to Austria consumed with the idea of developing a similar organization. In May of 1903, Moser and Hoffman succeeded in obtaining the financial backing of Fritz Warndorfer, a young art collector and banker, and the Wiener Werkstätte was founded with Koloman Moser and Josef Hoffman as artistic directors. Consisting of a series of individual workshops specializing in all phases of the decorative arts, the Wiener Werkstätte was dedicated to the harmonious incorporation of design elements, both from an architectural and an interior decor point of view. Koloman Moser, apparently restless in his search for artistic ideals, left the Wiener Werkstätte in 1906 to join a splinter group led by the painter Gustav Klint. From this point until his death in 1918, Koloman Moser's professional career remains shrouded in obscurity. Although Moser's departure had a significant impact on the design capability of the Wiener Werkstätte, new and talented artists continued to join and the organization flourished.

After World War I, the Moser firm became recognized as the foremost Bohemian producer of artistic glass and luxury tableware. Perfection in the glass medium and forming techniques, coupled with the work of highly skilled specialists in the fields of cutting and

---

[2]On October 22, 1814, the government of Winterberg submitted a request to the Piseker Regional Office for permission to build a glass manufacturing and cutting facility "for the Gratzener Glassmaster Josef Meyer" (1732–1829). Built on the site of an older glassworks founded by Count Adolf of Schwarzenberg, from which the glasshouse derives its name, the financial success of this undertaking brought welcomed prosperity to Winterberg. After Josef Meyer passed away, his favorite son, Johann (1775–1841), assumed control of the Adolf glassworks. Wilhelm Kralik (1806–1877), one of Johann Meyer's gifted glassmakers and trusted workers, married Meyer's niece Anna Pinhak in 1831. Josef Taschek (1814–1862), Meyer's nephew, later married Wilhelm and Anna's oldest daughter, Ferdinandea. When Johann died in 1841, Wilhelm Kralik and his son-in-law Josef Taschek merged the glassworks of Adolf, Eleonorenhain and Kaltenbach into the largest single firm in Bohemia, known by the name of Meyr's Neffe (Meyer's Nephews). In 1854, Meyr's Neffe acquired the glass hollowware factories of Ernstbrunn and Franzensthal. At a later date, Idathal and Louisenhütte, located in close proximity to the Adolf works, were also purchased. After Josef Taschek's death, Wilhelm Kralik managed the entire Meyr's Neffe complex. At this time, Meyr's Neffe was known as one of the foremost Bohemian producers of high quality glass products. This reputation, in addition to the marriage between the daughter of Josef Lobmeyr, Louise, and Wilhelm Kralik in 1851, prompted Ludwig Lobmeyr to entrust Meyr's Neffe with the production of a new style of Renaissance-type glassware in the late 1860s; this close and profitable relationship between J. & L. Lobmeyr and Meyr's Neffe was maintained for many years. Approximately four years after Wilhelm Kralik's death in 1881, the original firm of Meyr's Neffe was subdivided among his four sons. Karl and Hugo Kralik (died 1883) retained the Adolf glassworks at Winterberg, Idathal and Louisenhütte, as well as the name of Meyr's Neffe. After Karl Kralik's death, his sons Rudolf and Albert became co-owners of Meyr's Neffe.

---

[3]Extensive research has uncovered no direct relationship between Ludwig and Koloman Moser.

Fig. 12 Cut punch bowl and glasses designed by Jan Kotêra and executed by the Count Harrach Glassworks, Nový Svêt. Initially designed around 1903 with an engraved frieze but simplified after 1910. Collection of the Prague Museum of Decorative Arts (inventory no. 14170).

engraving, resulted in a flood of individual production orders intended primarily for exhibition purposes. In this regard, Moser executed designs for the professors and pupils of the School of Applied Art in Prague for exhibition at the 1925 International Exhibition of Decorative Arts in Paris. One of these pupils, Hana Dostálová, exhibited a magnificently cut and engraved jardiniere which later won a prize in another Parisian competition. Engravings produced by Hana Dostálová are now sought by discriminating art collectors all over the world. Another pupil, Ludvika Smrêková, destined to become one of the most famous Czechoslovakian

artists, submitted designs which, according to one reference, were never realized in glass form. Moser also cooperated with the Munich Deutsche Werkstätte and executed large facet-cut vases designed by Wolfgang V. Wersin.

Several notable glass artists/designers worked independently at the Moser factory during the latter half of the 1920s. These artists were responsible for the production of large quantities of Unikati (one-of-a-kind) which stylistically represented a significant departure from the more classical Moser designs. Among these was Chris Lebeau, an internationally recognized Dutch graphic artist and designer, who was a visitor at the Moser factory from 1926 to 1929. Lebeau's work is characterized by the sensual melding of form, color and texture accented by the use of rim edging in contrasting colors (Plate 164). Heinrich Haussman, an acclaimed glass artist/designer from Liepzig, was invited by Leo Moser to produce artistic glass at Meierhöfen. Haussman's designs, executed during the 1925–1927 time frame, are characterized by the use of massive single layer or cased glass blanks (Plate 168) which have an abstract naturalistic motif accented by deep acid cutting. Haussman's glass is generally signed with the acid-etched monogram illustrated in Figure 91. Tyre Lundgren, known for his figural and decorative engraving of thin-walled vessels, was also actively involved with the Moser firm.

During the 1921–1923 time period, the Moser Glassworks established a commercial contact with the French Argy-Rousseau Glassworks. Negotiations involved a licensing agreement permitting Moser to produce small glass articles using the pate-de-verre technique. Although costly manufacturing preparations were apparently completed at Meierhöfen, pate-de-verre glassware was never actually produced by the Moser firm.

Wiener Werkstätte designed glassware produced by Moser was shaped with multiple facet-cut surfaces and featured richly colored glasses exclusively developed by Moser for the Wiener Werkstätte. Variants of this decorative style enjoyed considerable popularity during the 1920s and fall under the general category of "Fantazie"

Fig. 13 Close-up of "Maria Theresa" goblet showing finely detailed engraving. Moser factory photograph.

Fig. 14 "Maria Theresa" engraved table service (prod. no. 10620). Produced by the Moser Glassworks throughout a major portion of the first half of the 20th century. From the collection of the Prague Museum of Decorative Arts.

Moser. Cubistic Art Deco forms (Plate 176) were also produced for more than a decade. Moser continued the long established tradition of enameled glass decoration which permitted participation in the exhibition of painted glass held at the Arts and Crafts Museum in Prague in 1924. In response to Moser's display of decorated glass at this exhibition, Prague art critic Karel Herain wrote:

"The products of the Moser Glassworks are first class both artistically and technically. They penetrate into the elegant strata and adapt themselves to this task with refined taste and a sense for originality. The glassworks can be regarded as an exemplary enterprise, especially due to its cooperation with artists, founded on a specialized basis. The prosperity of the works proves the error of the opinion that Czech glassworks should base their production merely on the demands of the consumer."

Early in the 1920s, Moser was the first glasshouse to introduce a new line of colored glasses based entirely on rare-earth oxide colorants. Developed, in part, by Leo Moser, these exotic glasses exhibit dichroic-like characteristics (in the sense of dual colors; perceived color is a

Fig. 16 "Diplomat" table service, cut (prod. no. 25400). Designed after 1920, produced up to the present. Moser factory photograph.

function of glass absorption and background illumination). Uniquely suited to the established Modern and Art Deco cutting styles, products featuring these new glasses were awarded a gold medal at the 1925 International Exhibition of Decorative Arts in Paris.

In 1923, Leo Moser presented a 218-piece crystal drinking table service for 24 persons to Pope Pius XI. Each piece was finely engraved with the pontifical tiara. Cost was no object in achieving the highest possible quality; so delicate and exacting was this task that only four engravers in the entire factory were entrusted with its execution. In response to this presentation and the accompanying social reception, the following letter of appreciation was drafted at the Vatican and sent to the Moser factory:

From the Vatican
May 28, 1923

Staatssekretariat
S.H.
Nr. 18.315

Your Honorable!
You are probably well aware after the personal reception accorded you, the degree of pleasure with which His Holiness has received your artistically executed Crystal Table Service. The rare quality of engraving exhibited by this expensive gift evokes the admiration of His Holiness and gives the Holy Father reason for undivided and hearty praise.

Fig. 15 "Diplomat" water pitcher. Height 11". Collection of Tradewinds Furniture & Crystal.

The Holy Father would like to express a wish that you forward his feeling and admiration to all the other men of the famous Karlsbad Crystal Company that worked together with your honorable. His lively wish is also that his words of appreciation and thanks be conveyed to the hardworking workers that created this expensive work with artistic talent and exactness.

In as much as I forward to you the expressed wishes from the Holy Father, I also part with my expression of exceptional and high admiration.

Your Honorable bowing,
V. D. Gaspari, m.p.

The Honorable
Mr. Leo Moser

International publicity surrounding this presentation produced a flood of orders for duplicate sets. However, requested prices by potential customers were well below initial production costs. After much deliberation and an intensive analysis of production techniques, Leo Moser set up a production line in which several engravers were each given a tool designed to do a simple but specific task. Results of this innovation surpassed expectations and the rate of production was increased threefold without significant loss in quality. Demand remained sufficiently high that 30 men were occupied full time filling orders for the "Pope's" set.

In the late 1920s, the Moser firm further broadened its extensive association with independent German and Czech artists. Heinrich Sattler, who was a professor at the Werkschule in Cologne-on-Rhine, produced simplistic stylized figural and sport motif designs. Alexander Pfohl produced acid cut-back cameo designs for application to vase type forms while he was professor at the specialized school of glassmaking at Nový Bor. Pfohl produced designs for the Moser Glassworks well into the 1930s. Numerous figural designs for diamond-

Fig. 17 Leo Moser in the Vatican for the presentation of the Pope's drinking set.

Fig. 18 "Pope" table service, in honor of Pope Pius XI (prod. no. 11520).
Moser factory brochure; collection of Tradewinds Furniture & Crystal.

point (stipple) engraving were generated by the painter Hilda Zadikow-Lohsing (a native of Prague). Sand-blasted decorations were designed by the Imperial German Artist Nora Ortlieb. During the early 1930s, the artists Mariane Schoder, Bernhardine Bayerl and Irmgard Bohn designed forms and engraved decorations primarily for application to colored glassware.

As previously noted, over the years Moser glass became internationally known as the "Glass of Kings." While to some this title may seem somewhat pretentious, the list of wealthy and important people known to have purchased Moser glass is lengthy indeed. Moser was named supplier to the Royal House of Hapsburg and the King of England, and its customers included such notables as Edward VII of England, Queen Alexandra and Queen Elizabeth of England, Pope Pius XI, Emperor Wilhelm II of Germany, King Alphonso XIII of Spain, King Faud I of Egypt, King Zachir Mohammed Shah and King Amanullah of Afghanistan, Sultan Sidi Mohammed Ben Jussef of Morocco, King Haakon VII

of Norway, King Victor Emmanuel II of Italy, Czar Boris of Bulgaria, King Carol of Rumania, Prince Regent Paul of Yugoslavia, President Inskander Mirsa of Pakistan, President Asreirsson of Iceland, Emperor Haile Selassie I of Ethiopia, Sultan Abdul Hamid of Turkey, and the Shah of Persia.

Due to the high cost of acquisition and the educational level usually associated with appreciation of its finer qualities, luxury glass has a limited demand in any given geographical area. This marketing dilemma had been addressed by Ludwig Moser through his establishment of an extensive worldwide network of commercial outlets. It is not surprising, therefore, that when the Great Depression hit the United States in October of 1929, the resulting tidal wave of financial disasters which swept the world impacted heavily on the Moser firm. 1931 saw the collapse of the largest Austrian and German banks. In 1932, the Moser firm experienced severe financial difficulties which led the Bohemian Union Bank to propose that the value of stockholders'

Fig. 19 Goblet from the "Lady Hamilton" table service. Made for the Maharajah of Travancore (prod. no. 15000/OP). Moser factory photograph.

Fig. 20 "Lady Hamilton" table service, cut (prod. no. 1500). Moser factory brochure; collection of Tradewinds Furniture & Crystal.

shares be reduced to 20 percent of their original value. A desperate attempt was made by Leo Moser to regain financial stability by introducing several new lines of low-cost art glass. Unfortunately, due to financial pressures beyond his control and the malignant environment surrounding the Nazi rise to prominence in Germany, this effort was destined to fail. In 1933 the Adolf works at Winterberg was sold. That same year witnessed the severance of the Moser family from the company founded by Ludwig Moser 76 years earlier; the remaining Moser brothers sold their corporate shares to the Bohemian Union Bank.

Leo Moser left Meierhöfen shortly after the brothers' corporate shares were sold. Richard, however, chose to remain with the firm for an additional three years; later, he accepted a position in Prague as the resident manager of a Swiss based merchandising firm. The manifest artistic and technical contributions of Leo to the success of the Moser firm have been reasonably well recorded. Of considerable importance was Richard's adroit organization of international exhibitions and his ability to move freely in the elegant strata of European society. Possessed of musical talent, Richard attended the Vienna Conservatory as a young man and was an accomplished pianist and flutist. His pleasing countenance and engaging personality won him many influential friends. Among these were the King and Queen of England, who, during the 1920s, were instrumental in Richard's appointment as British Vice Consul to the spa towns of Marienbad, Franzenbad and Karlsbad.

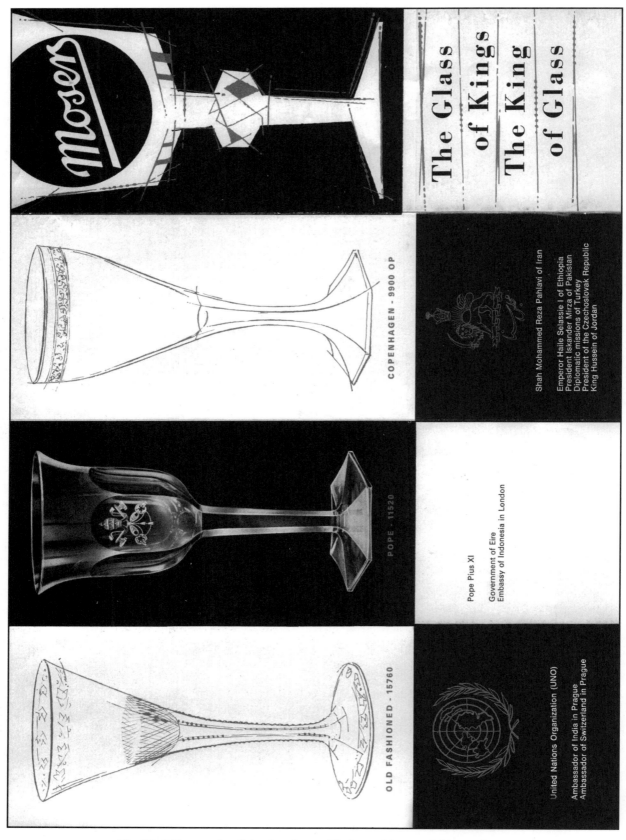

Fig. 21 A Moser advertising brochure of their most famous table services.
Collection of Tradewinds Furniture & Crystal.

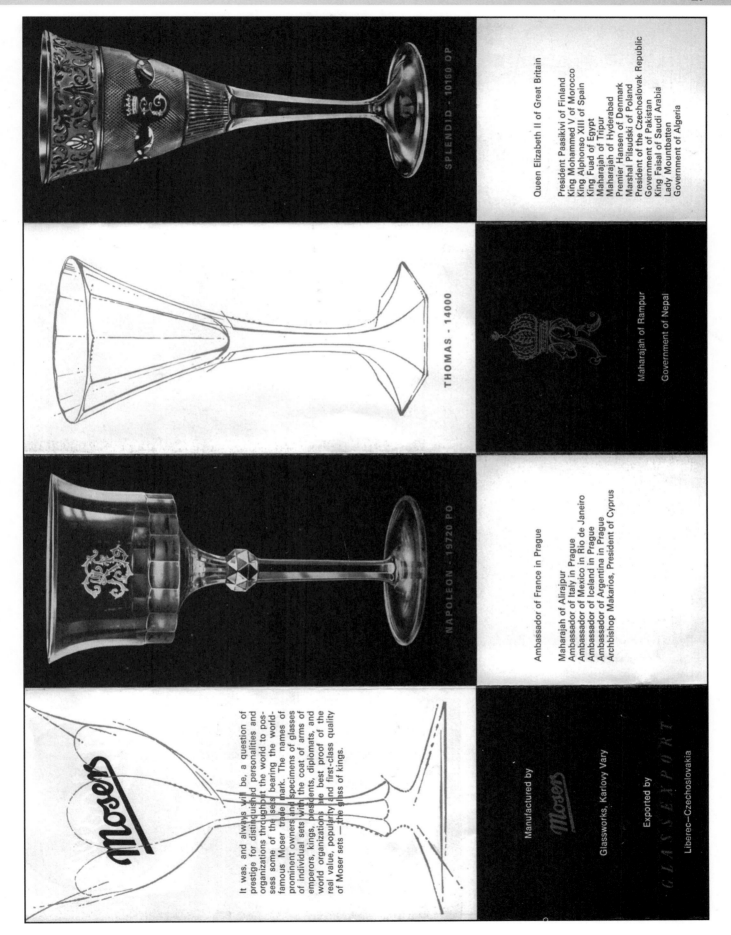

SPLENDID - 10160 OP

THOMAS - 14000

NAPOLEON - 19720 PO

It was, and always will be, a question of prestige for distinguished personalities and organizations throughout the world to possess some of the sets bearing the world-famous Moser trade mark. The names of prominent owners and specimens of glasses of individual sets with the coat of arms of emperors, kings, presidents, diplomats, and world organizations are best proof of the real value, popularity and first-class quality of Moser sets — the glass of kings.

Queen Elizabeth II of Great Britain

President Paasikivi of Finland
King Mohammed V of Morocco
King Alphonso XIII of Spain
King Fuad of Egypt
Maharajah of Tripur
Maharajah of Hyderabad
Premier Hansen of Denmark
Marshal Pilsudski of Poland
President of the Czechoslovak Republic
Government of Pakistan
King Faisal of Saudi Arabia
Lady Mountbatten
Government of Algeria

Maharajah of Rampur

Government of Nepal

Ambassador of France in Prague

Maharajah of Alirajpur
Ambassador of Italy in Prague
Ambassador of Mexico in Rio de Janeiro
Ambassador of Iceland in Prague
Ambassador of Argentina in Prague
Archbishop Makarios, President of Cyprus

Manufactured by

Moser

Glassworks, Karlovy Vary

Exported by

GLASSEXPORT

Liberec—Czechoslovakia

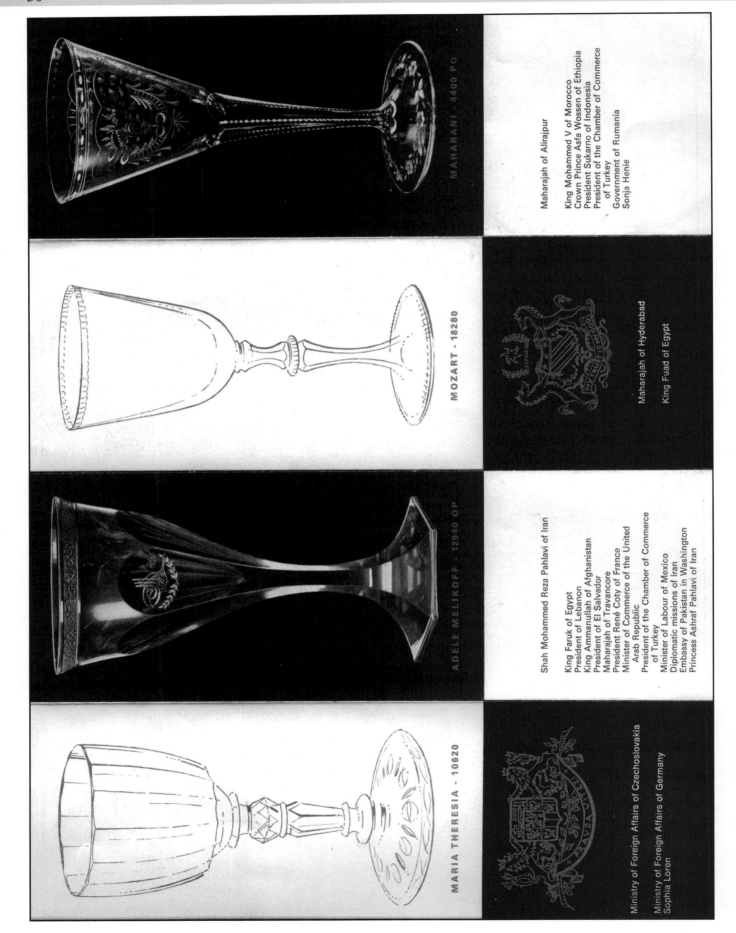

MAHARANI - 4400 PO

MOZART - 18280

ADELE MELIKOFF - 12940 OP

MARIA THERESIA - 10620

Maharajah of Alirajpur

King Mohammed V of Morocco
Crown Prince Asfa Wossen of Ethiopia
President Sukarno of Indonesia
President of the Chamber of Commerce
    of Turkey
Government of Rumania
Sonja Henie

Maharajah of Hyderabad

King Fuad of Egypt

Shah Mohammed Reza Pahlavi of Iran

King Faruk of Egypt
President of Lebanon
King Ammanullah of Afghanistan
President of El Salvador
Maharajah of Travancore
President René Coty of France
Minister of Commerce of the United
    Arab Republic
President of the Chamber of Commerce
    of Turkey
Minister of Labour of Mexico
Diplomatic missions of Iran
Embassy of Pakistan in Washington
Princess Ashraf Pahlavi of Iran

Ministry of Foreign Affairs of Czechoslovakia

Ministry of Foreign Affairs of Germany
Sophia Loren

ROYAL - 9000 POS

King Edward VII of Great Britain

Queen Alexandra of Great Britain
King Haakon VII of Norway
Sultan Abdul Hamid of Turkey
President Celal Bayar of Turkey
President Assgeirsson of Iceland
Generalissimo Stalin
Maharajah of Baroda
Maharajah of Navanagar
Diplomatic missions of Czechoslovakia
National Assembly of Guinea
Embassy of Philippines in Canberra

RIO - 9900/9000 PO

King Mohammed Zahir Shah of Afghanistan

Diplomatic missions of Brasil

LADY HAMILTON - 15000 OP

Shah Mohammed Reza Pahlavi of Iran

King Mohammed V of Morocco
Maharajah of Travancore
President of Chile

ARGENTINA - 16400

Diplomatic missions of Argentina

Ambassador of Italy in Buenos Aires
Crown Prince Asfa Wossen of Ethiopia
Ambassador of Ecuador in Chile

Fig. 22 The "Adele Melikoff" table service, cut (prod. no. 12940). Moser factory photograph.

Fig. 23 "Mozart" table service, decorated with pearl cutting (prod. no. 18280). Designed about 1935, produced up to the present. Moser factory photograph.

Fig. 24 "Napoleon" table service, cut (prod. no. 19720). Designed in the late 1930s, produced up to the present. Moser factory photograph.

Fig. 25 "Kristalit" table service (prod. no. 10900). Moser factory brochure; collection of Tradewinds Furniture & Crystal.

Fig. 26 "Argentina" table service (prod. no. 16400). Moser factory brochure; collection of Tradewinds Furniture & Crystal.

Shortly after the Sudetenland fell into Nazi hands, Richard met with his only son, Ludwig, in Prague for the last time. In a fatalistic yet prophetic statement, Richard declared his belief that Europe was lost and, after bidding farewell, left Prague for South America. Ludwig was later interned by the Nazis and spent 42 months in various concentration camps. By the time Ludwig arrived in the United States in 1948, all contact with his father had been irretrievably lost. After the war it was rumored that Richard had settled in Sao Paulo, Brazil; however, the location of Richard's adopted home in the Americas and the date of his death remain ostensibly unknown.

After his departure from Meierhöfen, Leo Moser became the managing director of several glass factories owned by the largest glass concern in Bohemia, Joseph Inwald Ltd. of Prague. These factories, located at Poděbrady, Schutzendorf and Teplitz, specialized in the manufacture of hollow and cut glassware which was exported primarily to England, Australia, South America and the United States. While with Inwald, Leo introduced modernized machinery and improved manufacturing methods which substantially elevated the worldwide marketing position of the Inwald firm. Recognizing the danger Hitler represented to those of Jewish heritage, Leo obtained American passports for his wife, Paolo, and son, Thomas. When his wife and son departed for the United States in June of 1938, Leo's daughter, Lea, chose to remain with her father in Europe. In August of 1938, after Hitler's bloodless annexation of Austria and before his conquest of the Sudetenland, Leo Moser and his daughter fled to France.

In France, Leo contacted his brother, Monsieur Gustov Moser, a French citizen of Medaille Militaire, Croix de Guerre, who, for 42 years, had been proprietor of the Moser sales outlet in Paris at 30 Boulevard des Italiens. While in Paris, and prior to his 1939 appointment as director-designer at Cristalleries de St.-Louis, Leo was repeatedly employed as a technical consultant to several large French glasshouses. In addition to being a noted designer of cut glass, Leo Moser was intrigued by improvements in manufacturing machinery and techniques capable of increasing productivity without sacrificing quality. These interests, coupled with extensive experience in the area of Bohemian glassmaking, were profitably employed at St.-Louis. A considerable body of dated and signed cut glass designs were generated by Leo during his tenure with this firm. Many of Leo Moser's designs were executed and marketed by Cristalleries de St.-Louis.

Concurrent with his acceptance of a position with Cristalleries de St.-Louis, Leo and his daughter Lea moved to the plant's location in the province of Alsace Lorraine. There they remained until the German invasion of the Low Countries in May of 1940. The flight of Leo and Lea Moser from the nightmare of Nazi terror represents but a somber echo of the crises which faced untold millions in the spring of 1940. Were it not for the magnanimous intervention of one of the truly great women of our time, their story might have ended in an entirely different fashion.

With the German invasion of Holland, Leo resigned his position with Cristalleries de St.-Louis and fled with his daughter to Nice where they obtained South American passports. In June of 1940, Lea and Leo boarded the ship "Alsina" at the port of Marseille. As fate would have it, France fell to the Germans on June 21 and soon thereafter the Vichy government compelled the Alsina to put in at the port of Dakar in the French North African colony of Senegal. After a period of approximately six months, during which time the ship's passengers were forced to remain on board, the Alsina sailed for Morocco. Upon arrival in Casablanca, the ship's entire complement was transferred to a concentration camp. With the capitulation of France, Leo's wife, Paolo, became justifiably concerned for the safety of her husband and daughter and appealed directly to Mrs. Eleanor Roosevelt for help. She was apparently quite successful. Based on a telegram issued on August 24, 1940, and undoubtedly initiated by Eleanor Roosevelt, temporary passports were authorized for Lea and Leo to enter the United States. In addition, Lea and Leo were mysteriously released from the Casablanca concentration camp and permitted to wend their way to Spain using any available conveyance. Traveling by way of Tangier and Seville, Lea and Leo arrived in Barcelona where they acquired U.S. passports. From Barcelona, the final leg of their journey took them to Lisbón, Portugal, where they boarded a Pan American Airlines plane for the United States. They arrived in New York in the spring of 1941.

From 1933 until the Nazi takeover of Czechoslovakia in 1938, the artistic glass output of the Moser works was primarily influenced by designs introduced prior to the departure of Leo Moser. Although the factory maintained a representation at international exhibitions, Brussels in 1935 and Paris in 1937, and continued to introduce new styles of cut glass, the worldwide market for artistic glass was in rapid decline. Under Nazi occupation, the board of directors was dissolved and all Moser stocks were transferred to the control of the German government. Renamed the "Staatliche Glasmann-factur, Karlsbad A. G., vormals Moser Karlsbad," the former Moser complex was converted to the production of items essential to the Nazi war effort. Many designers and artisans, who had previously been responsible for significant contribution to the world of artistic glass, were interned as political prisoners in concentration camps. Those who remained, worked virtually as slave labor although, their labors were not entirely without reward. By deliberately altering melt ingredients and proportions, workers managed to produce tank windows and filter glasses which mysteriously cracked or shattered prior to their arrival at the front.

Early in 1945, on orders of the Nazis, the factory furnaces were extinguished. In May of that year, nine of the original factory workers joined to rebuild the ovens, and, on September 1, their efforts proved successful. Although the Moser works found itself in the Russian Zone at the end of World War II, an extensive reconstruction program, directed at regaining the works' former splendor, was systematically pursued by the Czech government. This program was highly successful, and the Moser works is now known under the name of the "Karlovarské Sklo" glassworks. Even though a significant portion of the artistic glass produced by the Karlovarské Sklo glassworks is based on the designs of important contemporary artists, its major output still relies heavily on glass designs executed prior to 1933. The continuing commercial success associated with these products is an undeniable tribute to the elegant and timeless beauty of the artistic glass realized under the directorship of the Moser family.

PARTIAL LISTING OF PARTICIPATION AND AWARDS AT IMPORTANT EXHIBITIONS

1860	–	Industrial Exhibition in Vienna
1862	–	World Exhibition in London *(Medal)*
1873	–	World Exhibition in Vienna *(Medal for Workmanship)*
1878	–	World Exhibition in Paris
1879	–	Industrial Fair in Teplice
1884	–	New Orleans
1889	–	Exhibition in Frankreich
1891	–	International Exhibition in Tasmania International Exhibition in Jamaica
1892	–	International Exhibition in Colombia Exhibition on the Isle of Man
1897	–	World Exhibition in Brussels
1900	–	World Exhibition in Paris *(Silver Medal)*
1902	–	1st International Exhibition of Modern Decorative Art in Turin Austrian Art Exhibition in London
1904	–	World Exhibition in St.-Louis
1905	–	World Exhibition in Liege
1906	–	German-Bohemian Exhibition *(Recognition Diploma)* Exhibition of Applied Art in Liberec *(Diploma for Workmanship)*
1910	–	Exhibition in Belgium
1915	–	Pacific International Exposition in San Francisco *(Medal of Award)*
1921	–	International Exhibition in California
1925	–	International Exhibition of Decorative and Applied Art in Paris *(Gold Medal awarded outside the framework of competition)*
1935	–	World Exhibition in Brussels
1937	–	World Exhibition in Paris

IV. Moser—World War II and Beyond

After World War II, the Communist government nationalized the glassmaking industry in Czechoslovakia. Approximately 50 independent glasshouses which were in existence after the war, consolidated into 15 firms. Moser Glassworks was one of the few firms permitted to operate independently. Glassmaking has traditionally represented a major portion of the Czech economic picture. Consolidation was one approach to countering the significant reduction in glass production which occurred as a result of the war. In spite of these economic pressures, Moser maintained its historical emphasis on producing only the highest quality handmade glassware and, as a result, the Moser firm is presently recognized as one of Europe's preeminent glasshouses.

As before the war, the major Czech glasshouses are still concentrated in the Bohemian region of the country. Major glassmaking centers are presently located in the cities of Nový Bor (Haida), Jablonec (Gablonz), Teplice (Teplitz), Karlovy Vary/Dvory (Karlsbad/Meierhöfen), Železný Brod, Harrachov (Harrach) and Liberec (Reichenberg) and are represented by such names as Moser, Crystalex, Preciosa, Antonin Ruckl and Sons, and Egermann. Many of the previous producers of fine quality Central European glassware, such as Pallme-König in Kamenický Šenov (Steinschönau), Wilhelm Kralik in Lenora (Eleonorenhain), Ernst Steinwald on Teplice, Josef Riedel in Polubný (Polaun), Adolph Zasche in Jablonec, Josef Rindskopf in Kovstany (Kosten), Carl Goldberg in Nový Bor, Ferdinand von Poschiner in Buchenau, and Fritz Heckert in Petersdorf (Silesia) have significantly reduced production or are no longer in business.

After the collapse of Communism in the fall of 1989, the Moser firm rapidly transitioned to a joint-stock company. Emphasis was placed on acquiring Czech capitol, primarily to protect the Moser trademark and traditions, and Moser employees were encouraged to become shareholders in the firm. The present Moser management, headed by Jiři Novák, is committed to maintaining the long standing Moser tradition of high quality, exquisite shapes, innovative decorative motifs, and perfect workmanship. As in the past, this commitment to quality has resulted in numerous prominent political and social personalities, both in the Czech Republic and abroad, purchasing Moser table services, drinking sets and decorative glassware. With the parti-

tioning of Czechoslovakia and the formation of the Czech Republic, Moser Glassworks was commissioned to produce drinking sets with new state emblems for the office of the President of the Republic. In addition, it was requested that Moser produce gift glassware for state presentation purposes.

Moser decorative glassware, with the exception of those styles associated with contemporary artists, is dominated today by glass forms and styles which were developed prior to WWII. Every year new shapes are designed and introduced and their commercial acceptability subsequently evaluated. If they are successful, they are added to the already extensive selection of forms which were generated during the 1910–1939 time frame. For instance, in commemoration of Mozart's 200th birthday a special "Mozart" collection, featuring motifs of Mozart's principal works, has been prepared for sale in Japan. Moser has also acquired several unique 18th century objects from England. These items will form the basis of a new collection of replicas for sale in the United Kingdom and the United States.

Fig. 27 Věra Lišková, glass with engraved heron (prod. no. 2609). Designed in 1950. Height 7⁷/₈". Moser factory photograph.

After WWII, emphasis was placed on producing contemporary as well as traditional glassware designs. Contemporary designs were developed in cooperation with recognized Czech artists such as Věra Lišková, Ludvika Smrêková, František Zemek and Oldřich Lípa; all graduates of the Academy of Applied Art in Prague.

Věra Lišková explored the subtle nuances of thin-walled shapes in colored glass and designed engravings, and graceful but simplistic tableware services. She also specialized in facet-cut and shaped colored glass forms, such as animal sculptures, which remained in production for many years.

Ludvika Smrêková, concentrated on panel-cut vases of unique form drawn from her years of design experience. František Zemek designed vases with an emphasis on the plasticity and optical properties (i.e., refraction and dispersion) of the glass medium.

Oldřich Lípa joined with the Moser firm in 1955 and was responsible for a number of commercially successful designs. Initially he concentrated on designing sets of vases, which featured a fine matte decorative motif, as well as drinking glasses. Later, this earlier design work formed the basis of emotionally moving abstract designs which were engraved by Ivan Chaloupka. Many of these engravings featured musical themes. These four artists were instrumental in opening a new chapter in the already diverse palate of Moser glassware designs. This new look was so successfully represented at the World Exhibition in Brussels in 1958 that the Moser firm was awarded a gold medal.

Fig. 28 Věra Lišková, thin-walled decorative vases of blown crystal and colored glass *(left to right:* prod. nos. 1251, 1254, 1255 and 1252). Moser factory brochure; collection of Tradewinds Furniture & Crystal.

Fig. 29 Věra Lišková, Drinking set with air bubble (prod. no. 26640).
Moser factory brochure; collection of Tradewinds Furniture & Crystal.

Fig. 30 Oldřich Lípa, bar service (prod. no. 27060-80). Moser factory brochure; collection of Tradewinds Furniture & Crystal.

Fig. 31 Oldřich Lípa, set of heavy tumblers (prod. no. 27100).
Moser factory brochure; collection of Tradewinds Furniture & Crystal.

Fig. 32 Oldřich Lípa, cut vase with engraved figural motif (prod. no. 2012-V061). Height 11". Moser factory photograph.

Fig. 33 Oldřich Lípa, vase with cut and engraved abstract motifs (prod. no. 2012-V061). Height 11". Moser factory photograph.

Adolf Matura, Pavel Hlava and Vladimir Jelínek, of the Institute of Interior and Fashion Design, have been continuous contributors to the Moser design forum. Adolf Matura has been instrumental in enriching the already world famous Moser repertoire of rare-earth doped glass designs. Table services and plainly cut hollowware designed by Matura typically reflect a historical Modern design emphasis (Plate 196). Pavel Hlava is responsible for designs which emphasize highly decorative objects characterized by dramatic changes in glass color and complimentary cutting techniques.

Vladimir Jelínek concentrates his efforts on the design of table services which reflect traditional Moser characteristics emphasized by strong structural lines and finely executed facet cutting. Jelínek also heads an advisory commission at the Moser Glassworks which is responsible for reviewing both historic and contemporary glass designs and advising the Moser management on new products which should be introduced.

Fig. 34 Vladimir Jelínek, the "Jubilant" set, cut (prod. no. 27680). Designed in 1980. Moser factory photograph.

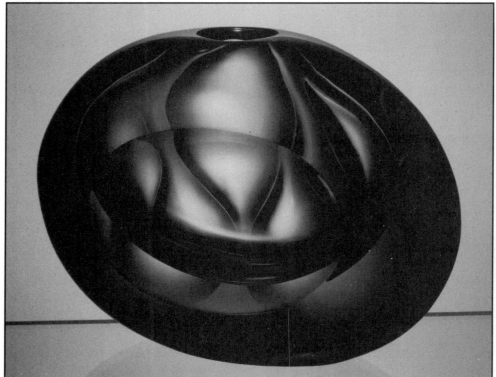

Fig. 35 Pavel Hlava (prod. no. 2210/3). Designed in 1974. Height 10³⁄₈". Moser factory photograph.

Fig. 36 Pavel Hlava, heavy vases of crystal and colored glass (prod. no. 54095). Moser factory brochure; collection of Tradewinds Furniture & Crystal.

Fig. 37 Vladimir Jelínek, the "Jadran" drinking set (prod. no. 27420). Designed in 1989. Moser factory photograph.

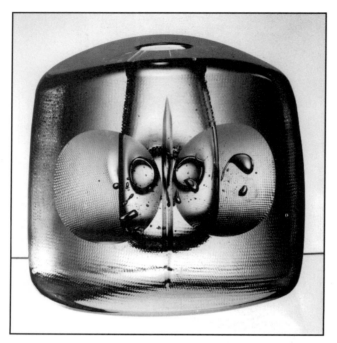

Fig. 38 *Left:* Vladimir Jelínek, crystal flower vase with air bubble optic and structural cutting, c. 1969. Height 8¼". Moser factory photograph; collection of Tradewinds Furniture & Crystal.

Fig. 39 *Below:* Vladimir Jelínek, decorative hand-cut candlesticks (*left to right:* prod. nos. 2223, 2224 and 2222). Height 5–5½". Moser factory brochure; collection of Tradewinds Furniture & Crystal.

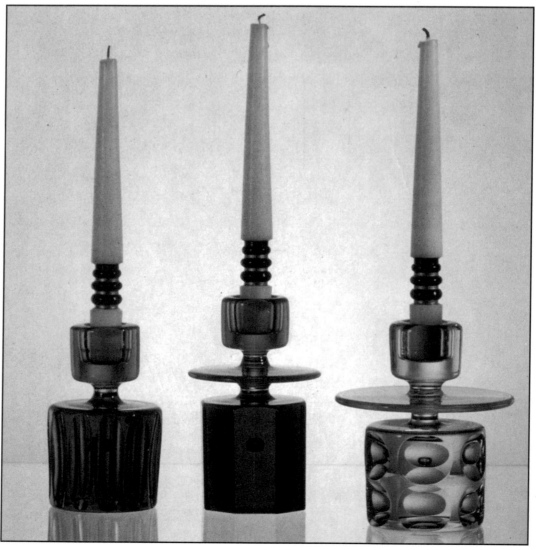

Fig. 40 Jiři Šuhájek, paperweight base glassware (prod. no. 27500). Designed in 1978. Moser factory photograph.

Fig. 41 "Fantazie" cut bowl in Bohemian crystal. Collection of Tradewinds Furniture & Crystal.

A distinctive contemporary design influence was introduced to Moser glassware via the efforts of Jiři Šuhájek. Through the fusion of two or more colored glasses, accented by facet cutting, Šuhájek created striking optical effects (Plate 197). In addition to the use of multiple colors to achieve contrast in a particular design, strong contrast was also achieved by combining heavy and thin walled glass in a single functional shape. A young artist by the name of Ivana Houserová designed a formal set of tumblers for the Moser firm which were highly regarded for their elegant simplicity.

Engraving, during the 18th century a primary staple of the Moser firm, is once again receiving the strong emphasis which it justly deserves. Although Moser maintains a large compliment of experienced engravers, younger people are continuously being added to the staff (training of novice engravers, from apprentice to master, generally requires a period of at least ten years). The primary engraving workshop at the Moser Glassworks is managed by a master engraver, Vladimír Skála, who retains responsibility for executing the most exacting designs. In addition to the primary engraving workshop, Moser has recently established a second engraving studio which specializes in designs based on historical or period graphic art and painting. Here, glass blocks are engraved with transposed (i.e., engraved on the back surface for viewing from the front) compositions which have their design basis in Renaissance art forms or in the works of modern artists. This Studio employs a small group of select engravers to include Luboš Metelák, Ivan Chalupka (Fig. 44) who is considered the preeminent Moser engraver in experience and capability, and Milan Holubek. Two highly qualified artisans, one specializing in cutting and the other in grinding, provide full service to the engraving Studio.

Luboš Metelák, who heads the Moser engraving Studio, joined the Moser firm in the early 1960s and is

Fig. 42 Ivana Houserová, paperweight base cut glassware (prod. no. 27660). Designed in 1980. Moser factory photograph.

still employed there. Metelák was successful in designing numerous tableware services (Figs. 43, 46, 47 and 48) which retained the traditional Moser ambiance while emphasizing a more contemporary presence. His designs also included facet-cut cased or single colored glass forms (Fig. 45) which featured engraved compositions (Fig. 44).

Historically significant artists, whose works have been transposed onto glass in the engraving Studio, include Albrecht Dürer, Michelangelo Buonarroti, Sandro Botticelli and Alfons Mucha. Dürer's grasp of form combined with a precision of style is reflected in

Fig. 43 Luboš Metelák, "Helena" cut table service (prod. no. 26660). Designed in 1968. Moser factory photograph.

Fig. 44 Luboš Metalák, composition engraved by Ivan Chalupka (prod. no. 2474/LM 164). Designed in 1985. Height 9⁷/₈". Moser factory photograph.

Fig. 45 *Left:* Luboš Metelák, hand-cut decorative sculpture executed in Alexandrit (prod. no. 2096). Moser factory brochure; collection of Tradewinds Furniture & Crystal.

Fig. 46 *Below:* Luboš Metelák, "Flora" table service (prod. no. 27000/OL). Moser factory brochure; collection of Tradewinds Furniture & Crystal.

Fig. 47 Luboš Metelák, "Meteor" table service (prod. no. 27480).
Moser factory brochure; collection of Tradewinds Furniture & Crystal.

Fig. 48 Luboš Metelák, "Monika" table service (prod. no. 27440/1). Moser factory brochure; collection of Tradewinds Furniture & Crystal.

Moser's engraved rendition of his graphic sheet, *Riders in the Sky*. Present day Moser engravers, particularly Ivan Chalupka, are the equal of the best Czech engravers of past centuries. These qualities are aptly displayed in sculptural engravings which capture the nobleness of gesture and expression characteristic of Buonarroti's paintings. Likewise, the playful detail and gracefulness of the female form, as represented by Botticelli in his *Primavera*, as well as Alfons Mucha's Art Nouveau graphics have been portrayed in excellent detail by Moser engravers.

From a contemporary viewpoint, the drawings of Karel Bečvář, who worked for the Moser firm in the early 1980s, formed the bases for a series of technically exacting engravings executed on crystal blocks. These engravings, transposed onto glass by Milan Holubek, reflect Bečvář's freedom of design and his flair for anec-dotes (Fig. 49). Perhaps one of the finest works produced at the Moser Studio was designed and engraved by Jiři Harcuba in 1982. Harcuba engraved both sides of a glass block to give the illusion of two angels, sitting back-to-back, each playing a stringed base instrument (Fig. 50). Harcuba's mastery of the engraving art and his innovative application of that art are clearly evident in this work.

A unique curiosity of the Moser Glassworks involves the production of a series of drinking goblets executed in Bohemian crystal. These goblets, originally designed by František Chocholarý in 1956, are generally referred to as "Giant Snifters" and are produced in a variety of shapes, heights and volumetric sizes. In 1958, these snifters first appeared at the Universal Exhibition in Brussels were they received an EXPO 58 Gold Medal. It was the intent of Chocholarý that each goblet be a cus-

Fig. 49 "The Race" (prod. no. 2565). Designed by Karel Bečvář. Moser factory photograph.

Fig. 50 Jiři Harcuba, "Music." Block engraved on both sides (prod. no. 2376/1982). Height 6⅞". Moser factory photograph.

tomized gift to a specific individual and that its form represent one of the six physiological classifications which Chocholarý used to characterize the human race. From this basis arose the names Big Bertha, Potbelly, Moonface, Long Face, Long Legs and Slender Lady (Fig. 51). In addition to their unique shapes, each Giant Snifter was designed to produce a distinctive tone (or chime) when toasting and the center-of-gravity was carefully controlled so that the snifter could be rotated in the hand without loss of stability.

A collection of post-WWII "Fantazie" Moser and Hock (wine) glasses, imported into this country prior to 1980, is presented in Plates 191, 193 and 195. This glassware reflects pre-war design influences and is primarily fabricated using unique Moser glass formulae developed in the 1918–1930 time frame. As evidenced in these photographs, at least two of the rare-earth glasses, "Alexandrit" and "Royalit," were produced after WWII. These unusual glass types are still being produced by the Moser factory. Modern cameo friezes, which are marketed under the name "Sovereign" (Plate 182), employ the "Amazon Warrior" motif designed by Leo Moser in 1914. "Sovereign" Moser, produced after WWII, is not as deeply cut as pre-war examples.

Modern Moser glass is sold through selected retail shops in practically all European countries, Japan, Canada, the United States and Singapore. Perhaps the most widely visited Moser outlet is on the Na Příkopě street in the center of Prague. Moser also has two shops in the Karlovy Vary area, one at the factory and the other on the Colonnade, and is in the process of opening a new shop in the capitol of the Slovak Republic, in Bratislava. Efforts are presently underway to systematically place Moser glass in multiple outlets throughout the United States which specialize in luxury products. During the 19th century, Ludwig Moser recognized the marketing advantage of combining luxury glassware with high quality porcelain products. This marketing thrust is once again being pursued by the Moser firm in conjunction with the products of Wedgwood (England). Because of the commercial importance and popularity of Moser tableware sets, the Moser factory maintains a replacement service for all its customers.

Fig. 51 Giant Snifters designed by František Chocholarý in 1956. Moser factory photograph.

V. Moser Decorative Styles Historical Development

According to an account given in *Czechoslovakian Glass*, the familiar allegation that Bohemian glass production was directly influenced by Italian immigrants in the 16th century cannot be supported by reliable evidence. There is little doubt, however, that Italian artistic concepts were copied and embellished by Bohemian artisans and that the importance of early Venetian glass in forming a backdrop for later Bohemian decorative styles cannot be overemphasized. During the latter half of the 16th century, much Venetian glassware was imported into Bohemia. This influx precipitated the adoption of enameling techniques and styles around 1570 which, although applied to Central European type forms, were Venetian in inspiration. Baroque decorative styles were introduced into Central Europe during the early 17th century and continued to dominate glass design until the emergence of Venetian forms around 1730. Within this time frame, Bohemian Baroque styles were strongly influenced by Italian as well as French glassmaking techniques and decorative motifs. After 1710, French adaptations of Baroque themes, (which would lay a foundation for the later Rococo), in addition to Berain-inspired motifs,[1] were extensively employed by Bohemian glass engravers and decorators.

With the perfection of chalk glass in 1683, Bohemian designers were given access to an artistic medium capable of supporting innovative engraving at the highest design levels. Initial efforts at engraving this new crystal were uninspired; however, when deeper engraving techniques were applied around 1700, the quality of engraving improved rapidly. Symmetry and balanced proportions characterized Bohemian glass shapes during the first half of the 18th century. Panel faceting, a cutting technique designed to enhance visual appeal by taking advantage of the refractive properties of glass, was a dominant feature of Bohemian Baroque glass during this period. It is interesting to note that much 19th and 20th century Bohemian glass, and, in particular, enameled glass marketed by the Moser firm, was manufactured with panels as an integral part of the mold-blown body. This attempt to emulate earlier facet-cut glass added an additional decorative dimension which significantly improved appearance without requiring costly cutting techniques.

A particularly noteworthy form of Bohemian Baroque glass was what is commonly referred to as "Zwischengoldglas" or "double-walled glass." Based on ancient decorative techniques of probable Jewish origin, Zwischengoldglas (literally, "gold between glass"), or its silver counterpart, "Zwichensilberglas," was produced from the beginning of the 18th century and generally consisted of gold or silver foil, cut or etched to produce decorative patterns, sandwiched between two layers of glass for protection. Decorative motifs for Zwischengoldglas were strongly influenced by Italian Renaissance and Baroque styles. Figure 1 illustrates a small Zwischengoldglas tumbler, attributed to Ludwig Moser by the Moser family, where the design has been worked in gold leaf using techniques essentially indistinguishable from those employed on later "Venetian" style glassware.

Although enameled glass was unfashionable during the first half of the 18th century, a particular form known as "Schwarzlot" ("black lead") enjoyed wide acceptance with wealthy clientele. In Bohemia, Schwarzlot is associated with the work of Daniel Preissler (1626–1733) and his son Ignaz (1676–1741) and was executed on clear glass using a shaded transparent black enamel (Plate 202). Inspired by engraved glass styles, Daniel Preissler is noted for his reliance on Baroque decorative elements while Ignaz Preissler is associated with Grotesque and Chinoiserie (or Chinese-like) ornamentation.

Schwarzlot is also characterized by the complementary application of gilding and surface scratching to enliven details; on occasion, iron-red enameling was also employed. Toward the end of the 18th century, enameled decoration regained its lost popularity. During this period, however, enameling was mainly applied to souvenir items and often decorated by home decorators ("Hausmalers") operating at the heavily trafficked spa resorts. Although the decorative themes employed are not generally considered to be stylistically significant, they did provide a background for 19th century decorators. Several elements in particular are relevant to

---

[1] Berain, Jean, the Elder (1638–1711). Belgian-born painter, designer and engraver who was particularly skilled at adapting the works of earlier artists, in particular Raphael, to the contemporary Louis XIV style.

Noted for his delicate arabesques and finely executed grotesques, Berain's later work helped provide the basis of the Regency decorative form.

Moser's "Venetian" style glass. For example, bright enamel colors were employed to decorate tableware with a variety of motifs including crests, stylized settings containing people surrounded by a Rococo cartouche, roses, garlands and floral bouquets.

Perhaps the single greatest influence on Bohemian Empire Period glass arose from the studio of Friedrich Egermann (1777–1864). Egermann, whose artistic style featured detailed ornamentation as well as mythological and genre scenes, employed artists and artisans to create new glass types and decorative forms under his guidance. Predominantly known for the development of Lithyalin glass, the stylistic output of Egermann's studio, particularly with respect to the noted artist Alois Eiselt (Plate 4), stylistically served as an inspiration to Moser enamelists working in the latter half of the 19th century. Moser is known for the extensive use of insects as decorative highlights. This artistic form matured during the Empire period and was employed by the Egermann studio as well as by the Mistrovice engraver Florian Wander. Further influence was felt from France, where gilding and silvering of exquisite delicacy was applied to Opaline glass. Considered by many to be the finest work of its type ever performed, this latter art form consisted primarily of flowers, butterflies, insects and animals. The artist Jean Francois Robert is best known for his association with this decorative style.

With the termination of the Napoleonic Wars and an upsurge in middle-class prosperity, the Bohemian Empire style of decoration was superseded by the Biedermeier period (c. 1825–1845). Of Germanic origin and principally applied to furniture styles, the Biedermeier form precipitated a distinctive alteration in Bohemian glass design. Bohemian manufacturers concentrated on the development of vividly colored glasses, such as Hyalith, and uranium glasses, as well as engraved cased glass. Forms generally became massive with intricate cutting and engraving. Viennese Biedermeier style was typified by the work of Anton Kothgasser (1769–1851) and featured town and genre scenes, portraits and flowers; the use of lavish gilding was not uncommon. Plate 2 illustrates a lidded container dating from the Biedermeier period. The glass body of this example, heavily doped with uranium and of a yellowish-green coloration (Annagrün), is executed in a typical Biedermeier style with an eight-point miter-cut star on the base. Seven of the eight facet-cut sides have a raised circular panel (cabochon) enameled with fruit or insects surrounded by a Rococo cartouche. Were it not for the Biedermeier form, the finely detailed enameling on this

example could easily be attributed to Moser decorators.

Use of multicolored stained panels with engraved decoration was also characteristic of the Biedermeier style. The pitcher and covered box in Plate 3 are two examples, dating from the 1860–1880 time frame, which exhibit profuse floral enameling applied to stained panels of varying colors. Although, in the absence of a signature, it is difficult to establish an accurate attribution, the extensive use of gold and enamel in an intricate and restless floral design bears a strong resemblance to later documented Moser works.

After 1835, the resurgence of Second Rococo decorative styles in Europe partially displaced the production of Biedermeier glass in Bohemia. Rococo ornamentation, principally rocaille (rockwork), in conjunction with colors inspired by romantic painting was revived during this period. Prompted by French porcelain decorative themes, glassware was enameled with female figures in romanticized period dress or with portraits of beautiful women. Many items of this type were probably commissioned as portraits of prominent family members. Portraits were enameled on circular or oval opaque white glass panels fused to a transparent glass ground and were often accented by intricate ornamental gilded framing (Plate 8). Although most glassware produced in this decorative style was out of vogue by the 1970s, some examples, such as the portrait vase illustrated in Plate 9, were produced by the Moser firm during the latter half of the 19th century.

With the influx of the Second Rococo came the final ingredient for the development of two characteristic 19th-century Bohemian decorative forms. In addition to indigenous artistic styles, Italian Renaissance, as well as French Baroque and Rococo themes, became incorporated into an easily managed framework of artistic design. In order to differentiate these mature Bohemian styles from their parent fashions, the terms "Bohemian Renaissance" and "Bohemian Baroque" are often employed.

For about 30 years after the Biedermeier period, Bohemian glass appeared to exhibit little originality. When European and English styles changed to classical and neo-Renaissance forms in the 1860s–1870s, most Bohemian manufacturers retained Biedermeier and Second Rococo decorative themes. Under pressure from foreign competition and in the face of increased demand for Bohemian products abroad, the quality of manufactured glassware declined during the 1860–1870 period. Cased glass, employed for multicolor engraving during the Biedermeier, was superseded by less costly stained glass. A widespread adoption of commercialized engraving techniques reflected a significant reduction in overall quality. Much of the lower quality engraved stained glass, recognized by most Americans as "Bohemian," originated within this time frame.

During the 1870–1880 period, glass decorated by the Moser firm was beginning to exhibit the unique properties by which Moser enameled glass can be recognized. Prior to this time, little definitive information exists regarding the decorative styles employed by Moser enamelists. It is probably reasonable, however, to assume that in many instances early engraved and enameled decorative styles ran parallel to one another. From the founding of the company in 1857, designers and engravers employed by Moser relied heavily on past artistic styles: for instance, from Rococo masters such as A. Watteau, Boucher, and J. H. Fragonard. With the hiring of top-quality engravers, Moser engraving became characterized by precise and detailed execution of figural compositions, ornaments, small emblems and initials; these properties are quite evident in much of the enameled glass produced by Moser.

By 1870 a series of artistic revivals, inspired partially by nationalistic themes and partially by the formation of museum collections of antique glassware, began to influence Bohemian glass styles. Initial response to these revivals was the reintroduction of glassware with enameled decoration executed in 16th and 17th-century styles. This German and Bohemian neo-Renaissance glass remained popular from 1870 to 1890. Islamic style glass decoration was introduced by J. & L. Lobmeyr, Meyr's Neffe and Ludwig Moser during the 1870s. Characteristic Islamic artistic forms employ high density geometric motifs. The influence of this decorative form is quite evident in much of the Moser enameled glassware produced prior to 1890. Rather than emphasizing geometric designs however, Moser glass was dominated by naturalistic motifs. In 1878, Moser exhibited heavily gilded glass decorated with Japanese inspired floral motifs (Plate 64).

J. & L. Lobmeyr first displayed iridescent glass in 1873 and commercial production began at Neuwelt in Bohemia. Iridescent glass was exhibited by a large number of Bohemian factories at the 1878 Paris Exhibition. By 1879, a large selection of Bohemian iridescent and bronze glass was being exported to the United States.

In the 1890s, Bohemia produced large quantities of enameled glass decorated to resemble English cameo styles. By applying heavy enamel to acid-etched colored grounds, facsimiles were produced bearing a close resemblance to the English prototype. Marketed under the names of "Florentine Art Cameo" and "Lace de Boheme Cameo," these imitations successfully destroyed the demand for the more expensive English cameo glass. "Mary Gregory" style glass was produced extensively in Europe and large quantities were shipped to the United States. Plate 65 illustrates a Mary Gregory style vase marketed by Moser which exhibits heavy white enamel rim, neck and base banding executed in the style characteristic of English cameo designers.

World markets had attained a sufficiently high level of competitiveness by the 1880s that Bohemian glasshouses were forced to adopt the more advanced manufacturing techniques practiced in England and the United States. These technologies paved the way for the innovative Art Nouveau styles which later rose to international prominence. The Art Nouveau movement (called "Jugendstil" in Germany and "Secession" in Austria) was firmly entrenched in Bohemia by 1895. By far, the most extensively produced Bohemian product in this category was iridescent colored glass executed with techniques introduced by Louis Comfort Tiffany. Although initially produced and exhibited by Johann Löetz Witwe, iridescent art glass of this type was also manufactured by such noted factories as the Kralik glassworks in Lenora, Harrach in Neuwelt, by both glassworks in Košťany, and by the Pallme-König and Rundskoff factories. Colored iridescent glass of the typical "Löetz" type which can be attributed to Ludwig Moser is unknown to the author. Koloman Moser, however, independently executed designs for E. Bakalowitz Söhn which were subsequently produced by Löetz, Meyr's Neffe and the Rheinische Glashütten.

Engraved Art Nouveau glass was also popular throughout Bohemia. Based on floral themes, this form of engraving was generally executed on clear crystal. Perhaps the most famous product of the Moser factory was deeply engraved Art Nouveau glass produced using color-shaded blanks of high purity crystal. Gustav Pazaurek (then Director of the Industrial Museum of Liberec), who was a noted expert in Art Nouveau decorative forms, applauded Moser for this innovative approach to Art Nouveau design.

After approximately 1900, Moser introduced yet another Art Nouveau decorative form. This new style, known as "Karlsbader Secession Glass," was not particularly popular and was apparently produced for only a short period of time (Plate 135).

Although the Art Nouveau influence in Central Europe was actually on the decline by 1905, the outbreak of World War I erased all remaining vestiges of this artistic form. After 1918, new art forms, partially based on concepts formalized prior to the war and partially dependent on individual artists and design groups, were introduced. Shortly after 1900, a "Modern" (one facet of the "Vienna Moderne" movement; current 1895 to 1930) school of design was founded, with a Prague professor of architecture, Jan Kotêra, as its most influential Bohemian proponent. Based on Baroque cut-glass styles, Modern glass design stressed the architectural quality of glass shapes, their function and the optical properties of the base metal (Fig. 12). A spin-off of this movement, the Artel group of artists, introduced Cubism to furniture and ceramic design and, through the efforts of the architect Josef Rosipal, to glass forms. This latter group, although initially of little influence, formed the basis of the Bohemian Art Deco style which emerged after 1925. Moser artists interpreted the concepts of Kotêra by producing a new line of glassware which, according to factory records, fell under the general name of "Fantazie" Moser. This form of glass decoration, which emphasized facet cutting techniques designed to enhance and accentuate the jewel-like properties of the base metal, was produced in various forms by Moser well into the 1930s and is still being produced today. Rare-earth doped glasses, introduced after 1920, proved to be a perfect medium for the execution of "Fantazie" Moser designs. Articles produced using these unique glasses brought the Moser firm well-deserved international recognition.

As artistic director of the Moser firm, Leo Moser exhibited a high level of artistic and technical expertise. From his constant study of glass chemistry emerged the commercial practicality of rare-earth doped glasses, as well as an extensive palette of subtle glass colors eminently suited to the crystal-cutting styles which characterized "Fantazie" Moser production. In a more practical vein, Leo collaborated with scientists at the Kaiser Wilhelm Institute in Berlin to develop an unbreakable clear glass which was marketed under the name "Dural."

Always interested in techniques which could simultaneously cut production costs yet retain overall quality, Leo participated in the development of polishing and

Fig. 52 Unbreakable clear glass Moser tumbler signed "Dural." Height 3½", c. 1930. Collection of Mr. and Mrs. Harry Foreman.

cutting machines, as well as manual procedures, which could rapidly perform precise, repetitive operations. Molded glass, which heretofore had been produced in limited quantities, was introduced to a broader spectrum of artistic glass products. When the effects of worldwide depression produced a marketing crisis which threatened to precipitate a financial collapse of the Moser firm, Leo drew heavily on these innovative developments to stem the tide of bankruptcy. Unfortunately, a predictable shift in social emphasis toward functionalism and low cost destroyed a major portion of the luxury glass market, and the Moser firm remained at a bare subsistence level until the Nazi takeover in 1938.

After WWII, the reorganized Moser firm continued to produce glassware forms primarily designed in the 1916–1938 time frame. In addition, Czech artists contributed their talents to the design of contemporary glass forms which found worldwide acceptance. Engraving, displaced in importance during the Art Deco period of the 1920s–30s, was revitalized by the Moser firm and has proven to be commercially viable in today's marketplace. A continuing emphasis on quality of design and execution has established the Moser firm as the preeminent producer of luxury glass in Central Europe.

VI. Classification of Moser Decorative Styles

In order to facilitate the identification of individual examples and their associated time periods, Moser glass has been partitioned into generic categories based on prominent decorative features and/or techniques. Throughout its history, the Moser firm was not a noted producer of classical art glass which relies exclusively on free-blown form, surface texture and color for its artistic merit. Although individual artists, such as Chris Lebeau, influenced the limited production of art glass forms, the vast majority of items marketed by Moser must be listed under the general heading of decorated or artistic glass. Characterized by the extensive use of engraving, cutting and/or enameling, Moser artistic glass can be classified under the following major headings:

CUT AND ENGRAVED GLASS
- Engraved Glass
- Art Nouveau
- Cameo
- Cut Glass
- Rare-Earth Doped Glasses
- Wiener Werkstätte/Art Deco

ENAMELED GLASS
- Enamel-gilt Decoration
- German neo-Renaissance Glass
- High-relief Decoration
- Acanthus Ornamentation
- Aquatic Life Forms
- Venetian Style Glassware
- Large Floral Enameling
- Ungilded Enamel on Glass

MOLDED GLASS

CUT AND ENGRAVED GLASS
Engraved Glass

Engraving on glass was the artistic foundation upon which the Moser firm built its international reputation of excellence. Of all the techniques available to the glass decorator, engraving is the most difficult and time consuming; consummate skill is required in the creation of even the most seemingly insignificant monograms. Although Moser engraving is typically characterized by detailed and precise execution, it must be remembered that there always has been a considerable variation in skill even among Moser engravers. That variation, when coupled to a market rang difficult to identify unless associated with glass types which, by themselves, are typically related to Moser. Intricate floral and Baroque engraving, accented with gilding, was apparently produced in large quantities by Moser during the 1890 to 1920 time period.

Some of the most common engraving styles encountered are illustrated in Plates 50, 51 and 52. These examples combine precision cutting with engraving accented by applied gold. For the majority of gilded examples encountered, gold highlights were initially applied to the engraved surface using a cold application process (i.e., the piece was not fired after the gold was applied). This application technique ensured a precise demarcation between engraved and non-engraved surfaces which greatly improved the appearance of the piece. Occasionally, fired-on gold leaf was employed to cover engraved surfaces (Plate 87). Although considerably more durable than cold gold, the gold leaf tended to overlap the engraved/non-engraved boundary creating a somewhat sloppy appearance.

Fig. 53 Close-up of engraved bird on Karlsbader Secession vase pictured in Plate 135.

Fig. 54 Moser's engraved and facet-cut "Neptune Chalice" (prod. no. 20689). Designed circa 1910, height 8⅝". Moser factory brochure; collection of Tradewinds Furniture & Crystal.

Based on an original model in the Prague Museum, the goblet in Fig. 55 is engraved with a classical Bohemian woodland scene. This example bears a Lobmeyer and Moser signature, and was probably produced at Moser's Meyer's Neffe glasshouse during the 1920s.

Engraved and graduated cups, from which spa visitors could partake of the healing waters, remained a stable commercial enterprise throughout the years of the firm's existence. Figure 2 illustrates several engraved spa cups of traditional design.

Stipple engraving, executed using a sharp diamond or hardened steel-tipped instrument, was first introduced by Anna Roemers Visscher in Holland, circa

Fig. 56 Finely engraved goblet in a form marketed by J. & L. Lobmeyr. Probably produced at Meyr's Neffe after 1922.

Fig. 55 Designed by Stefan Rath after an original model in the Prague Museum, this Bohemian crystal goblet with baluster stem and engraved woodland scene is part of Lobmeyr table set No. 253 (still in production). Height 7³/₄". Signed with script "Moser" and engraved Lobmeyr signature, c. 1925.

1621. This technique found limited use in the decoration of glass during the 18th and 19th centuries. Plate 166 is a stipple engraved Bohemian crystal vase highlighted with transparent enameling. This rare example is signed with both an acid-etched and stipple engraved "Moser" signature, has a stipple engraved artist's diamond-shaped monogram and was probably executed between 1925 and 1935.

Today, engraving has once again established itself as a commercial staple of the modern Moser firm. Top quality engravers (refer to Chapter Four), certainly equal to the best engravers produced throughout history, are engaged in creating contemporary as well as historically significant works of art. Fortunately, modern Moser is generally signed with the contemporary Moser acid-etched signature. This feature greatly removes the uncertainty associated with earlier works.

Figs. 57 and 58 *Left:* Signed "Moser" engraved Bohemian crystal vase of a form attributed to the Riedel glassworks; dated 1920. Height 9¼". *Right:* Close-up of engraving on decanter illustrated in Plate 189.

Fig. 59 "Barok" engraved and facet-cut table service (prod. no. 18500).
Moser factory brochure; collection of Tradewinds Furniture & Crystal.

As a point of reference in assessing the intrinsic value of engraved glass, Emil Gasek, vice-director of Moser production in 1979, estimated that 50 to 60 hours were required to complete one goblet of the "Barok" dinner service (Fig. 59). At that time, a goblet was selling for $175.00.

Art Nouveau

Art Nouveau became popular in Central Europe around 1895 and dominated artistic styles for a decade. As a general rule, Bohemian engraved Art Nouveau forms emphasized floral motifs executed on clear crystal blanks; shaded glass was rarely employed. The mainstream of Moser Art Nouveau glass, on the other hand, is characterized by the application of engraving techniques, developed initially by seal and gem cutters, to the generation of deeply engraved floral forms on heavy, facet-cut, high quality, color-shaded glass blanks; although comparatively rare, clear crystal was also employed. Engraved decoration consisted of undulating asymmetrical compositions of stems, leaves and flowers, sometimes complemented by the addition of enameling, applied insects and berries, and rarely, gold. Wild roses, tulips, day lilies, peonies and irises were favorite artistic subjects. Drinking goblets in supple Art Nouveau forms resembling the calyxes (cup or chalice) of flowers were also produced (Plates 124 and 125). Various Moser Art Nouveau glassware designs were registered with Handals und Gewerbekammer at Cheb (1901, 1903, 1904, 1905 and 1906). In spite of this precaution, engraved Art Nouveau glass similar to that produced by Moser was marketed by Graff Harrach in Neuwelt and Feix's in Albrechtice.

In its most common form, Moser Art Nouveau deep-engraved glass exhibits a gradual shading from a clear base to a colored top. Many glasses of this type were constructed from five-cased layers with the heavy outer layer of clear crystal, on which the deeply engraved motifs were worked, constituting at least 95 percent of the total glass thickness (refer to Chapter Seven, section under Glass Composition). A thin intermediate layer of colored glass of variable thickness provided the shading. Glass colors developed by Moser soon after the opening of the Meierhöfen works, which primarily included deep shades of ruby, cobalt blue, emerald green and amethyst mauve, were employed for Art Nouveau glass forms.

Occasionally, Moser Art Nouveau designs were embellished by the application of heavy glass insets composed of one or more cased layers of glass. This decorative art form is normally referred to as "padding" or "marquetry." Insets were generally floral forms with carefully controlled outlines to accurately portray the element desired and were fused to the background metal when at the working temperature. After annealing, the insets were cameo cut in contrast to the deep intaglio cutting employed on the remainder of the piece (Plate 122). A high level of skill was required to produce marquetry and it was only marketed by a limited number of firms. Louis C. Tiffany (U.S.), Thomas Webb & Sons and Stevens & Williams (England), Graff Harrach (Austria/Bohemia) and Moser were major producers of marquetry glassware.

Around 1900, Moser introduced a new type of glassware characterized by the combination of red and green or violet glass insets, matte green enameling, heavy high-relief, gold-enamel stems and intaglio-cut insects and birds (Plate 135). Produced under the name "Karlsbader Secession," this new glass style retained the Art Nouveau essence but represented a definite break from the deeply engraved Art Nouveau crystal produced prior to this time. Karlsbader Secession type glass was manufactured in tableware as well as purely decorative items, and it is recorded that quantities were purchased for use by the royal family at Castle Ehrenfeld. A lack of popularity compared to that of deeply engraved Art Nouveau crystal, and occasional color bleeding encountered during the manufacturing process, apparently limited the production of Karlsbader Secession glass.

Cameo

Beginning with John Northwood's copy of the Portland Vase, which was completed in 1876, there was a steady increase in the popularity of cameo glass. It was not until the 1880s, however, that the advent of acid/wheel cutting (acid rough cutting combined with a wheel-cut final finish) and acid cut-back techniques increased the availability of cameo glass to the general public. Following an early English lead, Bohemian factories flooded the European and American markets with bi-level cameo designs produced rapidly with the aid of hydrofluoric acid. Around 1900 Moser produced limited quantities of acid/wheel cut cameo of exceptional quality. Plate 133 illustrates an acid-cut cameo vase which rivals the best examples of its type produced in France. This vase, constructed from three cased layers, bears a "Moser Karlsbad" cameo signature. Moser also produced a considerable quantity of traditional bi-level cameo using two color glass blanks (Plate 134).

In the area of cameo production, Moser's greatest

output consisted of articles having friezes (bands) of gilded acid cut-back decoration. When coupled with richly colored facet-cut Modern or Art Deco Moser glass forms, this innovative design concept represented a major artistic accomplishment. Its popularity was widespread and constituted a major product line throughout the 1920s. Tableware in the "Copenhagen" (prod. no. 9900) and "Splendid" (prod. no. 10160) patterns, which featured frieze borders, gained immediate acceptance in the highest levels of society. In 1919, this successful decorative style was patented at the Patents Bureau in Berlin. However, as with Moser engraved Art Nouveau glassware, the patent process did not prevent rival Czech firms from producing similarly decorated artistic glass. Glassware with acid cut-back friezes is known to have been produced by Carl Goldberg (Nový Bor), Graff Harrach (Harrachov), and Pallme-König (Kosten near Teplitz).

By far the most commonly encountered frieze pattern features gilded Amazon warriors on a gilded/enameled acid-cut background (Plate 140). Original artwork for this pattern is dated 1914 and was probably designed by Leo Moser; however, it is unlikely that any quantity was produced before 1918. After World War I, the Moser

B

A

C

Fig. 60 (a, b, c) Partial documentation of Moser cameo-frieze patterns: *Above*, close-up of decanter in Plate 142; *Above Right*, close-up of vase in Plate 143; *Right*, close-up of bowl in Plate 144.

Fig. 60 (d, e, f) Partial documentation of Moser cameo-frieze patterns: *Left*, close-up of top of covered vase in Plate 140; *Above*, close-up of middle section of covered vase in Plate 140; *Below*, cameo-frieze on large Radion glass bowl.

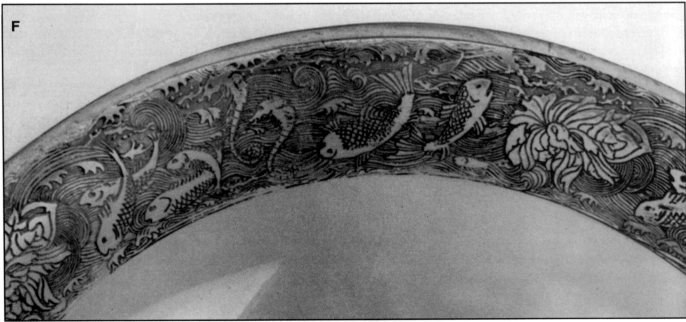

Fig. 61 Cameo medallion on Radion glass card holder.

firm produced additional acid cut-back gilded cameo patterns.

Frieze formats, used as borders, featured palm leaves, scrolls and cartouches. Most non-tableware cameo examples which fall into this category are signed with a diamond scribed "Moser Karlsbad" or "Moser Karlovy Vary" signature. Moser frieze type cameo frequently combines gilding and earth-tone enamels to accent the acid cut-back pattern. These enamels are employed within interstitial spaces where acid cutting has been employed to define a particular pattern element. Although the coloration added by these enamels is somewhat subtle, their presence is important in establishing a probable Moser attribution for cases where a specific article does not possess a valid Moser signature or known frieze motif.

As a passing observation, specific shapes of most Moser cameo-frieze glassware (excluding tableware sets) are not recorded in the two Moser line drawing books brought to this country by Leo Moser. These books are thought to cover the glass forms produced at Meierhöfen during the 1916–1930 time frame. A uranium doped vase, identical to that shown in Fig. 57, but without the engraving, is known to have been produced by the Riedel Co. Since Riedel specialized in facet-cut glassware similar to that found on Moser cameo-frieze forms, there is a possibility that most, if not all, of the Moser glass blanks destined for frieze decorations were produced at the Riedel factory.

Around 1925 Moser introduced the "Animor" and "Masken" series of acid cut-back cameo. Both of these series featured a wide cameo frieze on single colored or cased glass blanks. In contrast to the normally fully gilded narrow band type frieze, described in the previous paragraph, the highlights of the Animor and Masken decorative patterns are gilded while the acid cut-away background retains the color of the glass blank. Animor series cameo features animals in a naturalistic environment; elephants in a jungle setting is by far the most common pattern (Plate 159). Recently, an Animor vase was discovered with multiple African animals as well as an American bison. Masken series cameo employs a carnival-like grouping of figures as a decorative motif (Plate 160). Moser Animor and Masken series items are generally signed with a cameo "Moser" and "MK" signature and were only produced for a limited period of time.

Cut Glass

With the development of chalk glass around 1685, a medium of high clarity became available to Bohemian engravers and cutters. In addition to a rock crystal-like appearance, its inherent hardness permitted the use of decorative techniques heretofore reserved for stone cutting. Bohemian cut glass during this period was characterized by panel faceting combined with oval facets designed to enhance the elegance and brilliance of a particular design. Quite often, cutting was combined with engraving or enameling to achieve striking decorative effects. Prior to 1900, Moser employed cutting primarily as an adjunct to engraving or enameling. Early Moser styles were predominantly based on Biedermeier and Baroque themes which combined panel faceting, flute cutting and the use of raised oval panels, referred to as "cabochons" (Plate 60), with intricate engraved or enameled decoration.

During the Art Nouveau period, glass cutting gradually rose to new levels of importance, until, with the introduction of an extensive palette of colored glasses after World War I, cutting fully dominated Moser artistic styles. Shortly after 1900 a new concept in glass design, principally based on early Baroque cut glass styles, evolved in Bohemia.

Jan Kotêra, a professor of architecture at the Academy of Applied Arts in Prague, was the primary protagonist of this movement. Kotêra stressed the architectural characteristics of glass shapes, their functional properties and the optical quality of the metal. These principles were adopted by the Moser firm for the production of a new line of flawless, heavy cut crystal which empha-

sized the jewel-like properties of the glass medium. By concentrating on refractive and reflective effects created by carefully controlling glass thickness in conjunction with exacting facet cutting techniques, a style of sufficient universal appeal was developed whose popularity remains undiminished up to the present time. The majority of articles produced in this "Fantazie" Moser (or Modern) style are primarily characterized by a series of contiguous facet-cut vertical panels which follow the design contours of the piece. Plate 198 illustrates two facet-cut beakers which exemplify this decorative characteristic. A Moser developed spinoff of the Kotêra style featured wide, delicately outlined panels which were typically concave in form (Plate 170, top left). As recorded in Kunsthandwerk-Glas Holz Keramik (Sammiung Karl H. Brohan, Berlin, 1976), many designs of this type executed prior to WWII can be attributed to the artists Bayerl, Bohn, Ortlieb and Schoder. Leo Moser later referred to these designs as a form of "commercial art glass."

Fig. 62 *Above:* Facet-cut Pokal (covered goblet) in "Philadelphia" pattern (prod. no. 708). Moser factory brochure; collection of Tradewinds Furniture & Crystal.

Fig. 63 *Right:* An important deep amethyst Art Deco vase with a Renaissance style figural grouping executed in oroide (an alloy containing copper, tin, etc. used to imitate gold) and applied with a gravure photochemical printing process. Personally signed by Leo Moser, "Orogravur, Moser Karlsbad, Leo" and dated 1924. Height 11³/₈". Compliments of Mr. and Mrs. Harry Foreman.

Fig. 64 Deep amethyst facet-cut bowl in the Art Deco style. Signed "Moser Karlsbad," c. 1920–25. Height 5¼".

Fig. 65 Facet-cut vase in Oliv crystal. Acid-etched signature "Moser Karlsbad," c. 1925. Height 6½".

Fig. 66 Free-formed and cut examples of Moser glassware. Ashtray was a gift given by Leo Moser to his close friends at his 50th birthday party and is dated 1929. Vase is 7½" high. Collection of Mr. and Mrs. Harry Foreman.

Fig. 67 Gold Topaz Art Deco dresser set; a gift from Leo Moser to his daughter, Lea. The large bottle is 7" high. Collection of Mr. and Mrs. Harry Foreman.

Moser rarely, if ever, produced cut glass in the style which was popular during the American "Brilliant" period (circa 1876–1915), although elements of that form were sometimes employed to enhance, rather than dominate, a particular decorative motif. As an example, Plate 137 illustrates a Moser pitcher which combines the decorative features of diamond cutting and enameling on a shaded glass blank.

A vast majority of Moser cut glass has been marketed as tableware and it is through this artistic form, perhaps more than any other, that Moser glass has achieved and retained its high international visibility. Geometrically precise cutting, high purity crystal, delicately balanced design and intricately engraved or enameled monogramming are Moser trademarks; these characteristics are clearly evident in the "Royal" (prod. no. 9000) pattern wine service illustrated in Plate 148. In concert with the "Royal" pattern, the "Copenhagen" (prod. no. 9900), "Papel" (or Pope, prod. no. 11520), "Splendid" (prod. no. 10160), "Adele Melikoff" (prod. no. 12043), "Carlsbad" (prod. no. 13880) and the elegant "Thomas" (prod. no. 14,000) pattern tableware sets display the dominant facet-cut motifs which characterize Moser tableware.

As mentioned previously, cut glass, not designated for table use, falls collectively under the pre-WWII Moser designated classification of "Fantazie" Moser.

Fig. 68 Bohemian crystal Pedestal vase cut in the Modern style. Moser, c.1930. Height 10⅛". Collection of Mr. and Mrs. Ludwig Moser.

Rare-Earth Doped Glasses

Experiments performed by the German chemist Auer concerning the effects of introducing rare-earth oxides into a glass melt, in conjunction with the commercial availability of rare-earth oxides after 1920, led to the production of new and distinctive glass types by the Moser firm. These glasses were first produced in quantity by Moser and probably represent the culmination of a joint research effort by Leo Moser, Professor Quasebart of the Auer-Gesellschaft in Berlin, and Professor Turner of the English Glass Research Institute, Sheffield. Rare-earth oxides are relatively weak colorants; consequently, high concentrations are required to produce a reasonably dense shading. This fact, in combination with high material cost, limited the use of rare-earth oxides to fairly expensive artware.

As registered in the factory melt journals, Moser produced a multiplicity of rare-earth glasses. Those which actually appear to have been marketed are listed in Table 1. Many of these glasses are identified in Moser-related literature for the first time and the colors associated with several of them remain unknown to the author at the time of this printing. Alexandrit, by far the most common rare-earth glass, contains four to five percent neodymium oxide by weight and appears a pale bluish-violet under fluorescent illumination and red-violet in natural sunlight or under tungsten illumination (Plate 170). Heliolit, another important rare-earth glass containing neodymium and praseodymium, appears brown under tungsten illumination and green under fluorescent illumination (Plate 172). Royalit, a very costly glass to manufacture, was produced by combining neodymium oxide with selenium (Plate 169). Royalit does not undergo a dramatic color change when exposed to tungsten or fluorescent illumination.

Each of the rare-earth glasses exhibits the property of changing apparent color, depending on thickness and background illumination. This characteristic was exploited by employing special glasscutting techniques to visually enhance specific designs. Success in this effort is witnessed by the Moser firm's being awarded a gold medal at the International Exhibition of Decorative Arts in Paris in 1925 (this award was particularly prestigious since it was presented outside the framework of the established competition). While rare-earth doped glasses are generally found in the facet-cut Modern or cubistic Art Deco styles (with occasional decorative engraving), simpler hand-formed variations based on older styles can be found, such as the melon ribbed dresser box in Plate 170.

With the notable exception of Alexandrit, the majority of rare-earth doped glasses introduced and manufactured by Moser remain unique in the world of artistic glass. In the United States, the A. H. Heisey Glass Co.

TABLE I: Rare-Earth Glasses

DESIGNATION	RARE EARTH	COLOR
Alexandrit	Neodymium (Nd)	blue-violet to red-violet (Plate 170)
Alexandritbleiglas (lead glass)	Nd	blue-violet to red-violet
Didym (Ditit)	Nd, Praseodymium (Pr)	blue-gray
Heliolit (1)	Nd, Pr, Lanthanum (La)	unknown
Heliolit (11)	Nd, Pr	pinkish-brown
Heliolit W/119	Nd, Pr	pinkish-brown (Plate 172)
Latr W/89	Nd, Pr	pinkish-brown
Latr W/120	Nd, Pr	unknown
Latr 2/8.28	Nd, Pr	unknown
Latr P/1	Pr	unknown
Latr P/2	Pr	unknown
Latr P/3	La	unknown
Latr P/4	Pr	unknown
Praseamit	Pr	greenish-yellow
Royalit	Nd	brownish-red (Plate 169)

produced a glass which cannot be distinguished from Alexandrit when viewed under tungsten or fluorescent ambient lighting. After WWII, the Moser firm, along with several other Central European glasshouses, continued to produce neodymium doped glassware. Fortunately, a high percentage of post-war Moser Alexandrit is signed, which, in conjunction with its principal use for identifiable Moser Modern and Art Deco glass forms, aids considerably in establishing a proper attribution.

Wiener Werkstätte/Art Deco

Much of the Wiener Werkstätte's success can be attributed to the creative talents of its co-founder, Josef Hoffman. A professor at the Vienna School of Arts and Crafts, founder of the Wiener Werkbundes in 1912, an exhibitor at the Austrian Museum Exhibition in Vienna from 1911 to 1914, and a recognized leader in the design of silver, art glass and tableware, Hoffman exerted a dominant influence over most artists with whom he came in contact. Silver designs by Koloman Moser, Dagobert Peche (1887–1923) and Josef Hoffman are considered the quintessence of Art Deco form.

Hoffman's Art Deco designs, in particular, are noted for their distinguished and dignified character. Many glass designs executed by Josef Hoffman prior to World War I were subsequently produced by Moser. These works primarily served as the decorative elements for goblets, lamp shades, bookends and ornaments and consisted of facet cutting, as well as molded forms of animals, nude women and foliate decorations in opaque black and purple glass. Designs by Hoffman are usually signed "J. Hoffman" in engraved script on the base.

Over the years there were many Wiener Werkstätte designers involved with the production of artistic glass. Of these, only the names of a few of the most prominent will be mentioned. Machael Powalny (1871–1954) was co-founder with Berthold Löffer of the Wiener Keramik (ceramics), professor at the Vienna School of Arts and Crafts from 1909 to 1941 and a noted designer of Art Deco porcelain figures as early as 1914. Powalny preferred to work on a matte-finish glass surface which he decorated with primitive patterns and signs of the zodiac.

Dagobert Peche was a member of the Wiener Werkstätte from 1915 to 1923 and the director of its Zurich branch in 1917–1918. Peche specialized in simple floral motifs and, as mentioned previously, was considered one of the foremost designers of Art Deco silver. Otto Prutscher (1880–1949) was a student of Josef Hoffman and a professor at the Vienna School of Arts and Crafts. Prutscher designed cut, patterned and iridescent glass and was an important Viennese silversmith in the 1920s. Vally Wieselthier (1895–1945) became famous for his porcelain figurines produced by the Rosenthal factory. Additional artists and designers of note include Hilda Jesser (born 1894), Reni Schaschl, Mathilde Flögl, Leopold Bauer, Eduard Josef Wimmer (1882–1961), Julius Zimpel (1896–1925) and Fritzi Löw-Lazar (born in 1892).

Most of the Wiener Werkstätte designs produced by Moser can be recognized by their characteristic shallow "S" shaped bowls; this form is typified by the lightweight wedding cup in Fig. 69 and the heavier cut vase in Plate 179. Figure 70 is an excerpt from one of the Moser sketch books illustrating glass forms produced for the Wiener Werkstätte. A specific series of dark, richly shaded glasses was designated for Wiener Werkstätte's use in the Moser factory melt journal.

ENAMELED GLASS
Enamel-gilt Decoration

Gilding and enameling have often been combined to create decorative design elements. In this section, the term gilding (or gilt) will be used generically to refer to the use of gold, platinum or silver as the metallic compo-

Fig. 69 Stylized wedding cup in opaque black glass designed by Fritzi Löw-Lazar of the Wiener Werkstätte. Acid-etched "Moser" signature, c. 1930. Height 6".

nent of a decorative design.

One decorative technique, used extensively in Europe and the United States, was to outline the design element with gilding, fix the gilding in a muffle kiln, and then complete the design by filling in the element with enamel; a second firing fused the enamel to the ground. This technique is readily identified by the existence of well-defined boundaries between the gilding and enamel. A second decorative technique was to first lay down enamel to emphasize a design in relief. After the enamel was fired in a kiln, it was overcoated with gilding which was then fired to fix the entire design. Characteristically, this second technique completely overcoated the enamel; it is only through observation of the pattern from the reverse side that the existence of an enameled under-layer becomes obvious.

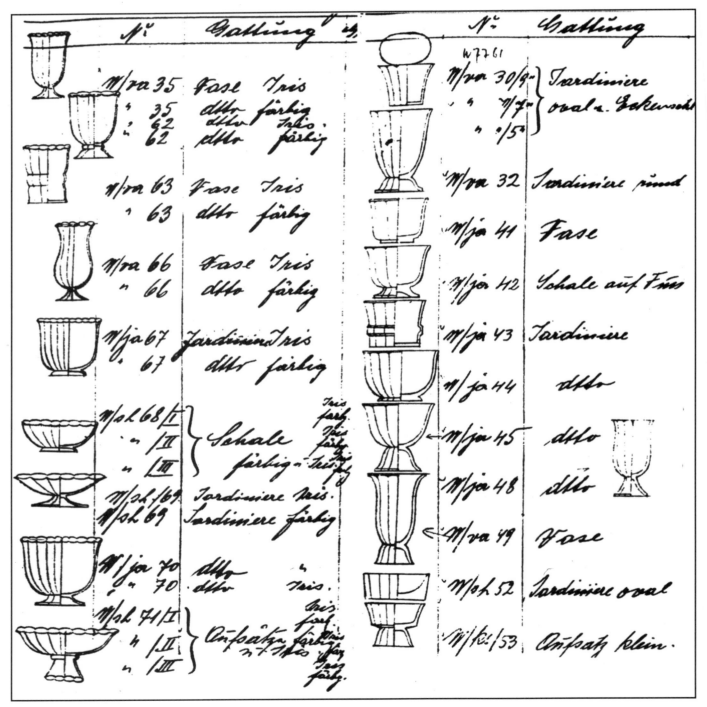

Fig. 70 Pages from a Moser sketch book illustrating some of the forms produced for the Wiener Werkstätte.

A third technique was to lay down a combination of opaque enamel and gold (or platinum) and to fire them simultaneously in a kiln. As a result, the metallic component and enamel mixed during the firing process, eliminating any well-defined boundary between the two media. This latter technique, which is referred to as "composite enamel-gilt," was extensively, but not exclusively, employed by Moser decorators; however, all three variants can be found on Moser decorated glass.

Composite enamel-gilt appears to have been accomplished by applying an opaque enamel to the ground to be decorated and then fully or partially overcoating the enamel with powdered metal in a liquid suspension. For the application of gold, brown oxide of gold, or gold salt, was ground with a flux and mixed with gum water or, for best results, with oil of turpentine. During firing, the enamel exhibited a tendency to displace the metal at the high points of the design; the relative visibility of the enamel would depend on the distribution and thickness of the metallic overcoat.

For finely detailed elements, such as twigs or outlines, it appears at first glance that the enamel was initially applied over a metallic background. This, however, was generally not the case. Protrusion of enamel through the metal is a critical factor in identifying this decorative technique, and, at times, careful observation is required to recognize this characteristic. Distinguishing between gold and enamel is made more difficult since yellow and orange enamels were generally employed with gold. Other colors, such as lavender, generally used with platinum, and aqua were also used, but such combinations are comparatively rare.

Moser extensively employed 24k high-luster gold for such decorative highlights as rim and body banding and interstitial patterns. Matt gilded surfaces were generally created by applying metallic leaf with a fixative, such as honey, to the ground. After firing, the metal would exhibit a matte finish which could be burnished with agate or blood stone to restore various degrees of luster. Moser decorators applied gilding to untreated glass, acid-etched glass and glass which was first coated with a thin layer of transparent enamel.

Matte and high-luster finishes were employed in similar capacities; however, matte gold and platinum were particularly used as pattern fillers, for example the interior of leaves or flowers which were outlined in composite enamel-gilt. The higher durability of these matte finishes, due to their greater initial thickness, made them an ideal ground for further decoration, and they were employed in that capacity more frequently than their high-luster counterparts. When gold or platinum leaf was employed as a ground (silver was rarely employed by Moser decorators because of its tendency to blacken due to oxidation), it was fixed in a kiln prior to the application of additional decorative elements. As a result, the glass visually exhibits a uniform coating when viewed from the reverse side. Composite enamel-gilt was apparently applied to a metal ground by using the same techniques employed for its direct application to glass.

Because of its softness, pure gold applied to glass is easily removed by abrasive action. For this reason, even limited use of tableware is evidenced by partial removal of gold, particularly on lip rims. A moderate loss of gold is not uncommon on gilded items and generally does not affect the value of a particular piece. Heavily worn examples should generally be avoided by collectors.

Transparent enamels were occasionally used in conjunction with composite enamel-gilt to achieve striking decorative effects (Plate 101). Elements formed by transparent enamels were generally outlined and highlighted in gold.

Reliable authorities agree that the quality of enameled decoration in Bohemia was in a state of decline by the turn of the 20th century. Due in part to an increased awareness of glass per sé as a unique art form, competitive pressures to produce glassware in ever increasing quantities compelled factory managers to search for decorative techniques amenable to mass production. Moser was not immune to this metamorphosis which produced a recognizable alteration in decorative styles. Prior to the opening of the Meierhöfen works in 1893, Moser enameled glass was characterized by the production of ornate and intricate floral and Rococo themes which fully covered the glass blanks to which they were applied. In many cases, decorative forms reflected prevailing artistic styles indigenous to the North Bohemian area surrounding Meistersdorf. Glassware produced during this period is highly sought after by contemporary American collectors.

As recorded in *Bohemian Glass* by Robert and Deborah Truitt, Julius Mühlhaus opened a decorating workshop in Nový Bor in 1870. Mühlhaus purchased only the finest glass blanks produced by Harrach, Meyr's Neffe and Löetz for his decorative efforts. Museum exhibits of Mühlhaus' decorative glass indicate that intricate composite enamel-gilt patterns emphasizing naturalistic elements were produced by this firm. In general, glassware of this type is virtually indistinguishable from similar ware produced by Moser. Considering the geographical proximity of the Moser and Mühlhaus factories (Moser in Meistersdorf and Mühlhaus in Nový Bor), in addition to other interesting comparative factors outlined in Chapter Eight, there appears to be a strong likelihood that Moser contracted Mühlhaus to produce composite enamel-gilt glassware to support product demand. There is also the interesting possibility that the two firms remained as independent competitors.

From about 1895 to the start of World War I, enamel-gilt decorative patterns, while retaining the essence of previous floral and Rococo designs, became abbreviated in form. Rather than forming a totally dominate artistic expression, enameling began to complement the glass forms to which it was applied (Plate 109). With the conclusion of World War I and the relative economic stability provided by the Bohemian Union Bank, a definite refinement in enameling techniques became evident. While still retaining earlier artistic elements, decorative patterns became light and fresh in appearance, and there was a noticeable improvement in technical execution (Plate 147). Much of this change was undoubtedly related to the purchase of Meyr's Neffe Adolf glassworks in 1922. Consideration of the decorative patterns, quality of execution and refinements in glass processing leads to the conclusion that enamel-gilt decorated glass marketed by Moser during the 1920s and 1930s equals or surpasses that produced during the 19th century.

German Neo-Renaissance Glass

After 1870, newly organized glassmaking schools, such as Steinschönau in 1857 and Haida in 1870, both located in northern Bohemia, advocated the return to earlier glass styles. This movement occurred when Bismark and the Prussian monarchy were engaged in the struggle for German unification and served to highlight the common historical bond which existed between the various German states. At that time, glass forms primarily copied 16th and early 17th century Central European Renaissance styles and were decorated with enameled patterns derived from 15th and 16th century Italian decorative arts.

Glass was typically green, yellow-green and, sometimes, clear in color and was decorated with prunts, multicolored enamel beading, coats of arms, kings, knights, hunters and hunting emblems. In general, glass forms produced in Bohemia tended to be scaled-down versions of the originals or assumed contemporary shapes for functional purposes. Fritz Heckert (Silesia) is known to have produced accurate facsimiles of early Renaissance glass styles.

Full neo-Renaissance glassware was primarily manufactured between 1870 and 1890 and, apparently, in vast quantities. Harrach of Neuwelt, Meyr's Neffe in Winterberg and the studio of Ambrose Egermann (eldest son of Friedrich Egermann) were among the most noted producers of this glass type. Plate 74 illustrates a pair of Pedestal salts decorated in the German neo-Renaissance style; they are unsigned, but, from known provenance, were purchased from the Moser factory in 1880. As is characteristic of the vast majority of German neo-Renaissance glass, signed examples of Moser's work in this decorative style are unknown to the author.

High-Relief Decoration

High-relief decoration of a glass body can be obtained by applying heavy or multiple layers of enamel, fused beading, lamp/ovenwork or fused precast glass forms to the surface, or by attaching decorative elements with a low-temperature adhesive. Decoration of this type is recognized as being characteristic of the North Bohemian glassmaking centers surrounding Haida, Nový Bor and Steinschönau. Each of the above techniques was apparently employed by Moser decorators during the firm's tenure at Meistersdorf; however, the use of applied preformed glass acorns, grapelike clusters of glass beads, glass bodied insects and gilded metallic bees have become accepted as unique Moser trademarks. Although details are unknown, cast decorations were most likely produced by melting glass beads or powder (pate de verre) in a ceramic mold prepared using the lost wax process. Larger cast items were fused directly to the glass substrate prior to the application of decorative enamel. Smaller elements, particularly those used in quantity, were enameled or gilded prior to application. Cast objects are found in many varying forms which include birds, acorns, flowers, fish and aquatic forms, faceted jewels, insects, reptiles, leaves and grape clusters. Many of the more lavishly decorated items are found with precast elements in combination with lamp/ovenwork forms such as rigaree, stems, leaves, fruits and flowers (Plate 26). Glass beading was employed to form grape clusters and facet-cut glass provided jeweled highlights (Plates 38 and 49).

From the 1880s to the 1930s, Moser marketed a wide variety of jeweled glassware. It has been suggested that initially the majority of jeweled items were produced for the Russian market (Plate 49); after 1918, however, this market would have ceased to exist. Glassware of this type was decorated using glass jewels of various colors, sizes and shapes which were fused to the surround using enamels. In some instances the jewels were facet-cut to simulate precious stones. It was not uncommon for the applied jewels to be placed in an enameled and gilded jewelry-type setting.

One of the most sought after forms of high-relief decorated Moser glassware feature animals and/or birds in naturalistic settings. By applying a heavy gray enamel to the glass ground, Moser artists would sculpt a three dimensional image of the featured subject matter. After the sculpted enamel was fired in a kiln, the model received its coat of colored enamel and then a final firing. Plate 45 (Fig. 71) and Plate 44 (Fig. 72), respectively illustrate a high-relief eagle and robin in flight. Sculpting of a base enamel prior to its final colored overcoat was also employed to produce other decorative elements such as the high-relief Baroque scrollwork on the vase in Plate 47 and the grape clusters on the amberina pitcher in Plate 36.

Plate 103 illustrates an enameling technique employed by Moser decorators to create delicate floral forms in high-relief. Petals and complete flowers were individually formed and shaded prior to firing in a kiln. Evidence indicates that this decorative technique was introduced by Moser during the 1880s and was in continuous production into the 1930s. A page from a circa 1905 catalog, published by Carl Hosch (Nový Bor), illustrates a series of intricately enameled vases with apparent high-relief floral enameling executed in a style which could easily be attributed to Moser decorators.

Hosch utilized the services of numerous local refiners (decorators) to decorate their glass. Whether the examples sighted were actually decorated by Hosch artists is uncertain. During the 1920s and 1930s, several North Bohemian firms produced similar floral work and production continued at Nový Bor after World War II. A

Fig. 71 *Above:* close-up of sculptured enamel eagle pictured in Plate 45.

Fig. 72 *Left:* close-up of sculptured enamel robin pictured in Plate 44.

rather coarse rendition of this decorative technique, originating from Italy after World War II, is readily available on the American market.

High-relief floral decoration produced in Bohemia exhibits a continuous graduation in quality from exquisite early examples, largely produced in the 19th and early 20th centuries, to the more commercialized versions produced at Nový Bor after World War II. In general, it is extremely difficult to differentiate between high-relief floral decoration produced by Moser and rival firms. As a result, evaluation of this art form should be primarily based on its artistic merit and quality of execution.

As a possible aid in dating and identifying Moser glass, it is important to note that molded glass acorns, insects, flowers, etc., were generally attached to the glass ground with an opaque cream-colored enamel. These decorative elements were enameled only on their exposed sides. In contrast, applied bees (Plate 139) were not formed from glass, but rather were constructed using a lightweight plastic interior completely covered with a heavy gold-colored metal foil. Bees were attached to the base glass by means of a transparent low-temperature adhesive and are consequently more easily removed than their fused enamel counterparts. Based on the majority of decorative styles which either incorporate cast glass decorative elements or pre-formed metallic bees, it is generally accepted that cast elements were primarily employed prior to 1890 while the use of metallic bees came after that date.

Acanthus Ornamentation

A common thread linking all items decorated in the Acanthus Ornamentation style is acanthus leaf scrollwork executed in brilliant enameled colors (Plate 95). In some instances this foliate motif is combined with a repetitive series of half ovals defined by a matte-gold ground rimmed with white enamel and having centered enameled dots of varying color. Known as "Fish Scale," this latter decorative element can be found on 16th and 17th century Italian glass. Plate 204 illustrates a two-handled vase having a decorative pattern which combines the elements of acanthus scroll and fish-scale ornamentation. This vase was probably commissioned by J. & L. Lobmeyr during the 1880–90 period and was produced at Meyr's Neffe's Adolf works. A similarly decorated footed goblet is attributed to Meyr's Neffe in Ćeskísklo-XIX Stoleti (Plate 261). Page 261 of Historismus by Barbara Mundt illustrates a beaker and pitcher marketed by J. & L. Lobmeyr in 1873 which is heavily decorated with fish-scale ornamentation. These examples were probably produced by Meyr's Neffe.

Two examples of glassware combining acanthus scroll and fish scale decoration, which reside in the glass collection of the Passau Glasmuseum, confuse the issue of proper attribution. These examples, executed in green glass, are attributed to Graff Harrach and are virtually indistinguishable from the decorated examples illustrated in Plate 204.

Acanthus Ornamentation was apparently a rather popular decorative theme since, in addition to Meyr's Neffe and Graff Harrach, it was produced by Moser, the Riedel Glassworks and S. Reich & Co. Plate 97 illustrates a mounted vase combining Acanthus Ornamentation with a typical Moser vermicular decorative pattern. This vase, and the footed plate in Plate 95, are probably stylistically representative of the 19th century Acanthus Ornamentation produced by Moser. Moser decorators continued to employ Acanthus Ornamentation well into the 20th century.

Aquatic Life Forms

Aquatic life forms were a favorite theme of Moser decorators during the last quarter of the 19th Century. In general, such items produced by Moser can be characterized as possessing anatomically correct enameled and/or applied forms in combination with a glass color, texture and form which enhances the visual effect of an aquatic environment. Plate 48 illustrates several 19th to early 20th century examples of Moser aquatic glassware featuring enameled fish, storks and aquatic plants on an amber-stained crackle-glass blank. Stylized versions, which show a distinct departure from the more naturalistic forms (Plate 42), were also produced. Plate 43 features a brightly enameled salamander, in combination with glass insects, applied to a distinctive Moser simulated tree trunk-type vase.

Previously, it was thought that Moser was the dominant factory producing glassware decorated with aquatic themes. Recent research indicates that aquatic life forms were apparently so popular toward the end of the 19th century that a variety of glasshouses produced this type of decorative ware. Graff Harrach in Bohemia and Thomas Webb in England were dominant producers of aquatic life-form decorated glassware. Barbara Morris, in her book Victorian Table Glass and Ornaments also notes that Stevens & Williams and other Stourbridge (England) glasshouses produced aquatic theme glassware. It has been documented that applied ornamentations, such as molded fish, turtles, lizards, etc. were, at the very least, employed by Moser, Harrach and Webb. Examples of this decorative form produced by the aforementioned factories were of the highest quality and—without the benefit of a reliable signature—are extremely difficult to attribute accurately.

Venetian Style Glassware (c. 1900)

Common to the mainstream of what will be referred to as Moser decorated "Venetian Style" glassware is the use of a decorative motif composed of a gilded Baroque cartouche (known as "Graffito" in Italian), surrounding portraits or personages in 18th century dress, combined with bouquets and garlands of enameled roses (Plate 112). From a historical design standpoint, these decorative themes on Venetian style glassware are characteristically Bohemian.

Zwischengoldglas is an ancient decorative technique consisting of gold foil, scribed or cut by a sharp instrument to produce decorative patterns, sandwiched between two protective layers of glass. Plate 26 in *Czechoslovakian Glass* illustrates a Bohemian Zwischengoldglas plate, dating from the 1698–1710 time frame, which bears a striking resemblance to the hand-scribed gilded Baroque decoration present on Venetian style glassware. It is also documented that late 18th century Bohemian enameled tableware consisted predominantly of crests or stylized landscapes containing personages in period dress surrounded by frames of Rococo ornaments. During this same period, clear or opaque white glass decorated with motifs of roses, garlands and bouquets of flowers was quite popular.

A second decorative design appears quite often on Venetian Style glassware. This decorative form (Plate 115) represents an exact copy of a 16th century Spanish foliate and canine design and can be found applied to Bohemian as well as Salviati Co. (Murano) glass blanks.

Plate 117 illustrates two Jewish ceremonial goblets. Each goblet is constructed from Venetian glass; however, it is likely that they were intended for the Central European market. These examples were probably decorated by Moser.

In addition to these rather distinctive decorative styles, the glass employed for Venetian Style glassware was generally of Venetian (Murano) origin and emulated early Venetian refining and fabrication techniques. It is typically fragile, of excellent quality and light in weight. Footed items such as comports, goblets, etc., generally have folded-under rim bases; plates and bowls have applied circular cross-section base rims; and where pontil marks occurred they were normally left unfin-

ished. Mainstream Venetian Style decoration was generally applied to vibrant ruby red, green or cobalt blue colored glass blanks; although, lighter colored variants can also be found. Venetian glassware, featuring the foliate and canine decorative pattern, is typically of a light green or clear coloration. Venetian Style decoration is also found on Central European glass blanks. Central European blanks are heavier in weight, may be of cased construction and have a form which is characteristically Bohemian (Plate 118).

Before proceeding, it should be pointed out that ruby-colored glassware, decorated with the same artistic elements employed on Venetian Style glassware, was produced in Italy in the 1950s. This glassware can generally be differentiated from earlier examples by its wider variation in color (most examples exhibit an orange-red coloration primarily produced by a lower coloration density), lack of precise form (i.e., waviness in the rim or base) and the use of enamels with a medium to high gloss finish (enamels employed for Venetian Style glassware exhibit a flat finish). While earlier glassware was of consistent high quality, the quality of similar glassware produced after World War II varies widely.

Origins of the Venetian Style glassware presented in this book remain somewhat controversial. This subject is addressed in detail in Chapter Eight. While resolution of this problem may be of great importance to glass historians, it should be of little consequence to people who appreciate fine glass. Venetian Style glassware manufactured prior to World War I is of consistent high quality, can be found in a wide range of decorative variations and should be considered highly collectible.

Large Floral Enameling

After 1900, delicately enameled floral forms, Baroque and Rococo themes and lavish gilding partially gave way to decorative motifs dominated by flowering plants executed on colored or shaded glass blanks. A probable outgrowth of the deeply engraved Art Nouveau style, enameled examples generally lack the sinuous lines characteristic of the fully developed Art Nouveau form. Floral enameled glass in this category marketed by Moser was decorated by first using a stencil to outline the major design elements with a mottled gold enamel (not to be confused with gilding or composite enamel-gilt) after which the enamel would be fixed by firing it in a muffle kiln. After the first firing, the decorative pattern would be embellished with enamel and the piece would be fired a second time. This technique produced distinct boundaries between the outline and the shaded enamel filler. In addition to outlining, the gold-colored enamel was employed in many cases to provide a bouquet-like backdrop for the main subject. Typical backdrops were composed of finely leafed foliage or "Baby's Breath." In terms of variety of color, shading, size and general availability, vases and bowls decorated with enameled pansies must have enjoyed a high level of popularity.

It is important to note that Legras & Cie (France) marketed a line of enameled glassware under the name "Mont Joye" which is similar to that just described. Items of this type have also been found with a "Clichy" (France) signature. In addition, Graff Harrach has been singled out as a probable supplier of "Large Floral" enameled glassware.

Each of the Moser examples in Plate 138 exhibits near-identical glass fluorescence and glass construction characteristics. This indicates that glass blanks decorated with "Large Floral" enameling most probably had a common origin. Blanks are constructed from Bohemian crystal using three cased layers of glass and generally incorporate vertical paneling to simulate facet cutting. Although Moser was capable of producing glass blanks of this type, the forms under discussion represent a significant departure from the high quality Art Nouveau and Art Deco glass which was being produced at Meierhöfen at that time. Available evidence strongly suggests that the glass blanks employed for this decorative form originated from a Bohemian factory other than Moser.

Moser continued to function as a glass decorating house even after the Meierhöfen facility was established and it is probable that the enameled decoration on "Large Floral" glassware was applied by Moser artists. Although less likely, it is possible that the enameled decoration was applied at another facility and that Moser, as well as other companies, purchased the finished glassware and sold it under their own names. This practice was not uncommon in Europe during the late 19th and early 20th centuries. Definitive answers to the above intriguing questions remain unresolved at the present time.

Page 35 of Claude V. Cox's book *Ludwig Moser, Royal Glass Artisan, 1833–1916*, illustrates a clear aqua-shaded vase with gold aventurine flecking, enameled flowers, gold leaves and applied bees. Based on this example, the pair of vases in Plate 141 have been attributed to Moser decorators.

Ungilded Enamel on Glass

In this section we consider enameled subject matter which does not fall generically into the other decorative categories outlined in this chapter. Positive identification of Moser wares in this class, without the benefit of signed examples having similar or identical composition, is quite difficult. Production of ungilded enameled glass probably dates to the earliest days of the Moser firm and most certainly encompassed an extensive variety of decorative styles, many of which have yet to be identified. Of the limited examples included in this book, the signed, cased and cut enameled vase in Plate 119 is representative of a popular type of floral motif produced by several Bohemian, English and French glasshouses. Plate 46 illustrates a signed amethyst vase with mold blown high-relief enameled flowers and leaves. A pair of vases, shown in Plate 139, feature large yellow enameled roses. The Art Nouveau cup and saucer in Plate 101 is yet another example showing the diversity to be found in Moser enameled glass. Enameled decoration on the example in Plate 115 is essentially a direct copy of a foliate and canine pattern found on 16th century Spanish glass. As a general rule, this type of decoration was applied to Venetian Style tableware and is occasionally found bearing a Moser script signature. Moser is known to have marketed various forms of "Mary Gregory" style glassware; a typical example is illustrated in Plate 65. Mary Gregory style glassware of this type may well have been decorated by Mühlhaus for Moser.

Plate 167 illustrates two chargers which, because of their distinctive flamboyant enameling, have been included in this section. From the decorative themes employed, it seems likely that glassware of the type pictured was primarily intended for the Spanish market. Examples produced by Moser in the 1920s are typically artist signed in gold "Royo" or "Cire." Evidence indicates that decorative patterns quite similar to those produced by Moser were also produced by Spanish glasshouses. Based on present knowledge, those articles bearing the gold signatures referred to above can safely be attributed to Moser; unsigned examples have a less positive attribution.

MOLDED GLASS

It was not uncommon for major glasshouses of the late 19th and early 20th centuries to market molded glass items as an adjunct to their premium lines of artistic glass. In the eyes of numerous collectors, the recognition of molded glassware is eclipsed by the more glamorous and expensive art glass forms. However, it must be remembered that molded glass not only permitted the acquisition of artistically designed glass by those of lesser financial means, but also, in many instances, provided much of the monetary support required for more aesthetic endeavors. At what point in time the Moser factory at Meierhöfen commenced production of molded glass forms remains undefined. It is recorded that Moser marketed molded glass designed by Josef Hoffman prior to World War I. Judging from its relative unavailability, it appears likely that molded glassware initially represented but a small fraction of Moser's total artistic glass output. With the advent of the Great Depression, however, financial pressures to greatly reduce fabrication costs naturally increased the importance of molded artistic glass and led to the introduction of finely executed designs typified by the examples illustrated in Figs. 73 and 74.

Plate 208 illustrates a molded and facet-cut malachite glass "Bacchus" style vase. An identical vase has been isolated which included "Karlsbad, Austria" in its

Fig. 74 Composite Alexandrit-Bohemian crystal molded vase in the "Chipped Ice" pattern, c. 1930. Height 6⅝". Collection of Mr. and Mrs. Harry Foreman.

authentic, but unidentified, acid-etched signature. Contrary to popular opinion, this example proves that molded malachite glassware was produced in Bohemia prior to WWI (i.e., before 1914); however, a specific firm involved with its manufacture has yet to be identified. During the 1930s a large quantity and variety of molded malachite artistic glassware was produced by the firm of Joseph Riedel (Polubný) under the trade name of "Ingrid." Molded malachite glassware was also produced in the late 1950s, in the original molds. On quality finished pieces, it is literally impossible to differentiate between the earliest and latest examples. Multiple examples of molded malachite glassware have been found bearing a variety of acid-etched Moser signatures.

Although some of these signatures may be questionable, there remains a high probability that Moser did market this glassware at some point in time. It is unclear whether Moser Glassworks was actually involved in the manufacture of molded malachite glassware, or simply sold it under the factory's name. Molded glassware, formed by using the molds employed to produce malachite examples, is also available in clear crystal and neodymium-doped glass resembling Moser Alexandrit. However, the alexandrite coloration is less intense in the imitation than in the genuine Moser Alexandrit.

Fig. 73 Molded Moser vase in Bohemian crystal, c. 1930. Height 8⅜". Collection of Mr. and Mrs. Harry Foreman.

DATING AIDS FOR MOSER GLASS

For the reader's convenience, a tabulated aid for dating Moser glass has been included in this chapter. In using this table, it must be recognized that the time frame specified for a particular identifying feature is only approximate and that in some isolated cases, articles bearing this feature may actually have been produced at a time considerably at variance with that stated.

TABLE II: Dating Aids for Moser Glass Production	
1857–1862, 1945–present	Production was almost exclusively engraved or cut glass.
1862–1870	Some enameled glass was produced; emphasis still on engraved glass.
1857–1875	Biedermeier designs were produced.
1857–1900	Second Rococo/Bohemian Baroque styles dominated Moser production. These styles continued to be produced well after World War I.
1857–1895	Hunting and woodland scenes were popular themes for engraving.
1857–1900	Moser glass cutting styles emphasized panel faceting, flute and miter cutting, and raised oval panels (cabochons).
1870–1880	Production of Muslin glass.
1870–1890	Production of German neo-Renaissance glass.
1870–1895	Production of intricately detailed and lavishly decorated glassware based on Second Rococo/Bohemian Baroque and naturalistic themes.
1875–1885	Islamic, Chinese and Japanese style glass produced.
1875–1914	Production of iridescent glass.
1880–1895	Mary Gregory style decoration produced.
1885–1938	Wheel-cut and acid cut-back cameo forms; wheel-cut variant probably only produced during the 1885–1895 time frame; cameo in style of late Gallé and Daum Nancy produced around 1900; Amazon warrior frieze introduced after 1918.
1895–1910	Deeply engraved Art Nouveau and enameled Art Nouveau floral forms.
1895–present	Colored and clear crystal production at Meierhöfen emphasized perfection of the crystal mass.
1895–present	Clear crystal production dominated by Bohemian Crystal. Lead crystal was manufactured in limited quantities after 1920.
1895–1910	Venetian style glassware appeared on market.
1900–1905	Karlsbader Secession glass produced.
1910–present	Modern Style cutting techniques employed.
1910–1938	Cubistic Art Deco designs produced.
1910–1938	Large floral enameling forms produced.
1910–1938	Wiener Werkstätte designs produced.
1910–1938	Enameled glass reflected earlier themes but with modern overtones.
1914(?)–1938	Production of molded artistic glass.
1922–present	Rare-earth doped glasses produced.
1930–present	Production at Meierhöfen was primarily clear Bohemian Crystal.

VII. Central European Glass Characteristics

MOSER GLASSES AND
TYPES OF CONSTRUCTION

Artistic style and decorative execution are but one side of the coin in establishing the value of artistic glass. Without the basis afforded by technical excellence in glass refining, forming and finishing techniques, the finest artistic efforts would be like singing Verdi's "Aida" accompanied by the strident tones of a honky-tonk piano.[1] Just as the technical characteristics indigenous to a particular glass manufacturer have the ability to reinforce overall quality, these same characteristics can often times provide valuable clues as to the proper attribution of unsigned examples. In addition to the obvious properties of color, purity, weight and finishing techniques, fluorescence, induced by ultraviolet radiation, adds an important new dimension to the study of artistic glass. While the use of fluorescence to attribute glass to a specific manufacturer remains largely unexplored territory, its value in differentiating between glass types, determining the structural configuration of a glass sample, disclosing the presence of chemical stains or conditioning agents (i.e., prior to the application of gold, etc.), or isolating repairs, is well established.

Prior to 1892, Moser functioned solely as a glass decorating firm and purchased quality glass blanks from suppliers located throughout Bohemia. Within this logistic framework, acquiring particular glass colors and shapes of acceptable quality over a prolonged time period, such as would be required to market and support the sale of extensive multifunctional tableware sets, would have been extremely difficult, if not impossible. It was probably this consideration more than any other which drove Ludwig Moser to establish his own glass furnaces.

In contrast to the cut and engraved crystal which dominated Moser table service designs, enameled glassware was generally reserved for decorative or less utilitarian objects. The aesthetic appearance of moderate to heavily enameled glass is less dependent on glass quality (bubbles, stria, etc.) and nuances in color than engraved, cut or lightly gilded glass. Consequently, it appears that a significant portion of the enameled glass Moser marketed after 1895 continued to employ glass blanks purchased from outside suppliers, in particular from Meyr's Neffe's Adolf Works in Winterberg. With Moser's purchase of the Adolf works in 1922, the production of enameled glassware was apparently moved to that facility, where it remained until 1933 when the Adolf works was sold.

When the glass furnaces at Meierhöfen facility became operational in 1895, the Moser firm concentrated on the development and production of high quality crystal. Throughout its history, the Meierhöfen never wavered in its dedication to the production of the highest purity crystal or to the execution of cut and engraved designs which emphasized the gem-like quality of the crystal mass. With its opening, Ludwig Moser initiated an experimental program directed at improving the quality of existing formulations as well as developing new types of glass. A direct result of this initiative was the early introduction of new glass colors which included rich shades of ruby, cobalt blue, emerald green, amethyst mauve, yellow and brown. In shaded variants, these new colors formed the basis of the deeply engraved Art Nouveau glass for which Moser became justifiably famous.

Moser also produced a little-known form of rainbow colored glass (Plate 162) primarily composed of striated blue, yellow and pink glass; green and opaque white has also been reported. Rather than being a glass mixture, rainbow glass was constructed by the careful addition of colored glasses to a clear gather prior to expanding it to its final dimensions. Cased and enameled versions of Moser rainbow glass are considered rare.

After 1921, Beryl, a lovely turquoise colored glass obtained by using Ce-Ti yellow glass modified with Cu (Plate 180), and Eldor, a pure lemon yellow representing glass gold (Plate 187), were introduced. Of primary significance, however, was the development of rare-earth doped glasses of which Alexandrit (Plate 170), Heliolit (Plate 172) and Royalit (Plate 169) were the most widely produced. Plate 181 presents a partial palette of unique, highly refined Moser glasses developed primarily for Modern and cubistic Art Deco cutting styles; additional glass samples are in the possession of the Corning Museum of Glass. Table II lists the non-rare earth glasses given in the factory melt journal for which color samples are known to exist. These glasses represent only

---

[1] In using the term "glass refining," we are here referring to chemical purity.

37 types out of a total journal listing of 61. Lower to moderate color density glasses, such as those listed in Table III, were normally used in a homogeneous form (i.e., constant color throughout the glass thickness) to create a particular object. If a lighter or graduated shading was desired, the final glass blank would typically be of three-layer cased construction. Most of the glasses listed in the melt journal from which this tabulation was derived were developed after World War I. They can be found free-formed, cut or engraved; however, they are rarely found bearing enameled decoration.

After 1920, several variations of lead crystal were developed by the Moser firm; examples of this glass type are rare. Even when the emphasis shifted from colored to clear crystal around 1930, Moser production remained dominated by Bohemian crystal. Moser advertisements from the pre-WWII period actually emphasized the weight saving that could be realized by using Bohemian crystal in place of lead crystal.

Fabrication of cased glass is not only technically challenging and costly but requires considerable glass blowing skill to produce high quality examples. A particularly critical area in the fabrication of cased glass occurs when two glasses having different thermal expansion coefficients are fused together at a high temperature. If the difference in expansion coefficients is sufficiently great, stress created at the boundary layer between the two glasses during the cooling process will produce fracturing.

One technique which is quite useful in joining glasses with widely differing expansion coefficients is to sandwich a thin layer of glass, having an intermediate expansion coefficient, between the two primary glasses. With this transition layer, which is referred to as an

TABLE III: Non-Rare Earth Moser Glasses

NAME	COLOR	PLATE/REFERENCE SOURCE
Amethyst	deep amethyst	Plate 181 (top, third from left)
Beryl	pale aqua	Plate 181 (top, seventh from left)
D. W. Blau	moderate density bright blue	Plate 181 (top, fourth from left)
Giftgrün	moderate density green-aqua	Plate 181 (top, sixth from left)
Gold Topaz	gold amber	Plate 181 (bottom, third from left)
Lavendblau (dated 12/2/30)	moderate density lavender-blue	Plate 181 (top, fifth from left)
Lichtbryl (dated 11/10/30)	very pale aqua	Plate 181 (top, eighth from left)
L. W. Altgrün (dated 1/16/30)	moderate density olive green	Plate 181 (bottom, seventh from left)
Lmaragd	deep sea-green	Corning
Oliv	pale olive green	Plate 181 (bottom, sixth from left)
Ozeangrün	moderate density ocean-green	Plate 181 (bottom, eighth from left)
Proles	moderate density brown-amber	Corning
" "	moderate density lavender-brown	Corning
" "	moderate density lavender-pink	Corning
Radion	brilliant greenish-yellow	Corning
Ranchrot Light	moderate density pinkish-brown	Corning
Ranchroth	moderate density pinkish-brown	Corning
Ranchtopaz	moderate density gray-brown	Corning
Ruby (dated 4/12/29)	moderate density ruby red	Plate 181 (top left)
Rossgrün	brownish-amber	Plate 181 (bottom, fifth from left)
Stahlblaü	moderate density bright blue	Corning
Saphir	moderate density sapphire blue	Corning
Weinroth	pale lavender-pink	Corning
W89	light pinkish-brown	

expansion-matching layer, loss due to stress-induced fracture is much less likely to occur. Typically, intermediate glass layers of this type are only several thousandths of an inch thick. Establishing their presence requires the use of a short-wavelength ultraviolet lamp and clear access to a cross-sectional area of the glass sample.

Ruby-colored glass, which in its paler shades is referred to as cranberry glass, was probably the most popular glass produced by Bohemian glasshouses. With comparatively few exceptions, shaded (rubina) and cranberry-colored ruby glass marketed by Moser, as well as other Bohemian glasshouses, was of cased construction. Deep ruby-colored glasses produced at Meierhöfen, or Venetian Style ruby glass, were not cased. In general, cranberry and rubina colored glasses were constructed from three layers of cased glass; the outermost layer was clear Bohemian crystal, the intermediate layer was gold, ruby-shaded Bohemian crystal and the inner layer was a thin protective layer of Bohemian crystal. Plate 124 illustrates an Art Nouveau marquetry goblet, manufactured at Meierhöfen, which is of rather unusual construction; thick, pale ruby glass was used as the outer layer for both the bowl and foot, the interior of the bowl was cased with a thin layer of clear crystal and the two interior layers of the foot were alternately constructed from clear and ruby glass.

Several additional glass types are of particular interest. Bohemian variegated lemon yellow glass (Plate 33), for example, is constructed from three or four cased layers. The outer three layers, which, as one progresses toward the interior, are clear, clear streaked with opaque-white, and lemon yellow, are of approximately equal thickness. A thin glass layer, only visible under short-wavelength ultraviolet radiation, was sometimes applied over the lemon yellow glass. Shaded pale pink-amber to apple green glass, believed to have been made at Meierhöfen and illustrated in Plate 111, exhibits two cased layers of approximately equal thickness when viewed from the green end.

Examples of deeply engraved Art Nouveau glass, in the shaded variants clear amethyst, clear green and clear blue, reveal the presence of five cased layers of glass. A clear Bohemian Crystal outer layer, on which the engraved decoration was worked, comprises approximately 95 percent of the total glass thickness. This layer is followed, in order, by a thin expansion-matching layer, a graduated layer of colored glass, a second thin expansion-matching layer and finally a thin protective layer of Bohemian Crystal. Color shading in cased glass is pro-

duced by varying the thickness of the colored layer. Two such graduated layers, joined to maintain a constant wall thickness, were used to produce the double-shaded Art Nouveau vase in Plate 123.

Temperature colored amberina glass produced in Bohemia during the latter quarter of the 20th century (Plate 99) exhibits a rather distinctive coloration; the red portion is a dusky red while the amber portion is a greenish-amber. Although attractive in its own right, this color combination is distinctively different from the coloration exhibited by amberina glass produced in the United States. To be competitive with American glasshouses, Bohemian manufacturers produced amberina-colored glassware by casing a graduated gold-ruby layer with amber glass (cased, three-layer construction similar to that characteristic of cranberry glass). The coloration achieved using this technique closely approximated that of the glassware produced in the United States (Plate 100).

GLASS COMPOSITION AND FLUORESCENCE PROPERTIES

Three glass types have historically dominated European glass production: 1) Bohemian crystal, a potash-lime glass; 2) Venetian crystal, a soda-lime glass; and 3) lead crystal, a potash-lead glass. Geographically, production of Bohemian crystal is typically limited to the Central European area (i.e., Bohemia, Silesia, etc.), Venetian crystal is characteristic of Italian glass production, and lead crystal was produced primarily in France, Belgium, England and Scandinavia.

Prior to approximately 1850, Bohemian crystal was composed of 100–200 parts pulverized silica (sand), 10–18 parts calcium oxide (quick lime), 7–24 parts calcium carbonate (lime) and traces of arsenious acid and peroxide of manganese. During this same time period, Venetian crystal was composed of 60% silica, 25% sodium carbonate (soda) and 15% calcium carbonate. After 1850, these formulations were revised and improved. Table IV lists comparative crystal compositions of this later period, and Table V lists a detailed formulation of typical Central European lead crystal.

Glass fluorescence (i.e., the characteristic coloration exhibited by glass when exposed to invisible ultraviolet radiation) can be quite useful in differentiating between Bohemian crystal, Venetian glass and lead crystal. Consequently, it can be useful in isolating a general geographic area of origin. When evaluating whether a specific example is constructed from lead crystal or Bohemian crystal, its weight or ability to "ring" when

TABLE IV: Comparative Composition of European Crystal After Approximately 1850*

INGREDIENT	VENETIAN CRYSTAL % BY WEIGHT	BOHEMIAN CRYSTAL % BY WEIGHT	LEAD CRYSTAL % BY WEIGHT
SiO_2 – silicon dioxide (sand)	66.0	65.0	46.0
K_2CO_3 – potassium carbonate (potash)	5.3	21.0	18.0
Na_2CO_3 – sodium carbonate (soda)	17.0	5.6	2.1
$CaCO_3$ – calcium carbonate (lime/chalk)	11.0	8.5	2.1
Pb_3O_4 – lead oxide	—	—	27.0

Plus colorants, decolorants (i.e., manganese) and refining agents (i.e., antimony)

WARNING: UV radiation can damage the eyes. UV lamps should not be used without protective goggles which block UV radiation.

TABLE V: Typical Formulation of Central European Lead Crystal

INGREDIENT	WEIGHT PER BATCH	% BY WEIGHT
SiO_2	66 kg	46*
K_2CO_3	26 kg	18*
Na_2CO_3	3 kg	2.1
Pb_3O_4	39 kg	27*
$CaCO_3$	3 kg	2.1
$BaCO_3$	3 kg	2.1
$Na_2B_4O_7$	0.5 kg	0.35
As_2O_3	0.4 kg	0.28
KNO_3	2 kg	1.4

Different types of lead crystal were made primarily by varying the proportions of these.

TABLE VI: Fluorescent Colorations Produced by Dominant European Glasses			
UV WAVELENGTH	**BOHEMIAN CRYSTAL**	**VENETIAN GLASS**	**LEAD CRYSTAL**
SWUV (254 nm)	Intense powder blue	Whitish to whitish yellow	Intense blue tending toward blue-aqua
LWUV (366 nm)	Translucent yellow, yellow-green, green or orange	Pale translucent yellow to yellow-green	Pale powder white-yellow to white

tapped are, often unreliable measures on which to base a judgment.

Evaluation of glass fluorescence must follow a consistent set of rules. In order to observe the characteristic given in this book it is imperative that a two lamp ultraviolet (UV) source be employed; one lamp is optimized to produce radiation primarily at a wavelength of 366 nanometers and the other lamp produces radiation primarily at 254 nanometers. Each lamp is employed independently in evaluating glass fluorescence properties; i.e., long wave UV (LWUV—366 nanometers) and short wave UV (SWUV—254 nanometers). Single UV lamps (these are primarily LWUV sources) or lamps using a sliding filter to change the wavelength output of a single lamp will produce misleading results.

Table VI lists the characteristic fluorescence observed when Bohemian crystal, Venetian glass or lead crystal are sequentially radiated by SWUV or LWUV radiation. For Bohemian crystal and Venetian glass, the translucent colorations observed under LWUV radiation were the resulted from adding decolorants and refining agents to the melt. As time progressed, and the purity of raw ingredients increased, the intensity and coloration of the translucent fluorescence under LWUV radiation steadily changed. Today, Bohemian crystal produced by Moser exhibits a very pale yellow-orange coloration under LWUV radiation.

From approximately 1850 to 1930, most Bohemian crystal produced was based on a formulation developed at Meyr's Neffe. This glass type exhibits the fluorescent properties given in Table VI. After the opening of the Meierhöfen works, Moser engaged in the development of improved formulations of Bohemian crystal.

Engraved Art Nouveau glassware, for instance, exhibits the colorations given in Table VI; however, the blue fluorescence is considerably more pale than for glasses produced at Meyr's Neffe. As one progresses through the 20th century, the coloration of Moser's Bohemian crystal under SWUV radiation slowly transitions from pale blue to a strong whitish-yellow. In fact, the fluorescent properties of Moser's contemporary Bohemian crystal under SWUV radiation are quite similar to those listed for Venetian glass. For lead crystal, the coloration noted appears to be quite consistent for glass produced up to WWII and, for Venetian glass, up to at least 1960.

SUMMARY OF DISTINCTIVE MOSER GLASSWARE CHARACTERISTICS

Included below is a compilation of technical and design characteristics associated with Moser glass. Some of these are typical of high quality Bohemian glass in general, while others are more intimately associated with Moser glass in particular. Venetian style glassware is unique and quite different from other types of Moser-related glasses; typical characteristics indigenous to this glass type are listed separately.

Mainstream Moser Glassware

• Concave polished pontil mark or flat polished base; exceptions include mold-blown and formed articles not requiring the use of a pontil rod.

• Double chamfered rim (both edges); exceptions are fire-polished rims (rarely used) or articles with applied rim decoration.

• Gilded rim (not a unique Moser characteristic); exceptions are deeply engraved Art Nouveau, Modern, Art Deco and German neo-Renaissance glass.

• Extensive use of mold-blown paneled glass for enamel-decorated ware.

• Generally heavyweight crystal; however, on a per volume basis, clear Moser crystal is considerably lighter than most contemporary crystal due to the absence of lead in the melt.

• Lavish use of gilding (both platinum and gold) when appropriate to the style of an article.

• Shaded and ruby (cranberry) glass is generally constructed from three to five cased layers.

• Limited use of lead crystal; no known examples prior to 1918.

• After 1895, glass intended for cut or engraved decoration is of flawless quality.

• Facet, miter and panel cutting executed with high mechanical precision.

Venetian Style Glassware
• Rough but recessed pontil marks from solid pontil rods.

• Folded-under foot construction.

• Applied circular glass rims on plates and bowls.

• Lightweight glass
  — Fire-polished rims
  — Gilded rims generally applied only on dark colored glasses
  — Highly refined glasses in deep rich tones of ruby, cobalt blue and green; also light colored glasses, amber and blue being typical, which emulate early Venetian glass styles.

Plate 1 Disassembled Zwischen-goldglas tumbler attributed to Ludwig Moser. Height 3³/₄", c. 1870. Collection of Mr. and Mrs. Harry Foreman.

Plate 2 Biedermeier Annegrün (uranium doped) tankard. Height 7¹/₂", c. 1840.

Plate 3 Early Moser type decoration, circa 1875 est. Pitcher on the right is 7⁵/₈" high.

Plate 4 Partial garniture set, Egermann studios; 19th century. Original work attributed to Alois Eiselt, 1815–1820.

Plate 5 Cameo and intaglio engraved vase of traditional Bohemian design. Unsigned. Height 13½", c. 1870–1880.

Plate 6 Punch set heavily decorated in gold and platinum; Moser. Bowl is 12" high, c. 1885.

Plate 7 Enameled and gilded urns; glass blanks are of traditional Bohemian aqua-opalescent glass. Moser. Height 12³/₄", c. 1885.

Plate 9 Portrait vase; signed "Moser, Glasfabrik, Karlsbad." Height 10¹/₂", c. 1875. Collection of Mr. Ronald Pugliese.

Plate 8 Bohemian portrait vases were not produced after approximately 1980; unattributed. Small vases are 10" high, c. 1840–70.

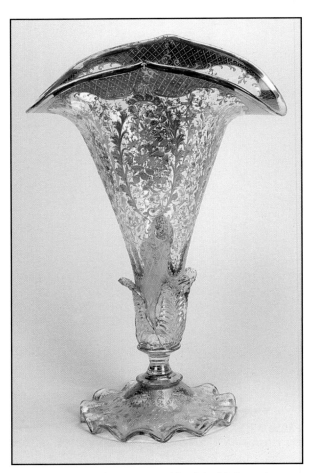

Plate 10 Decanter set decorated in heavy enamel. Moser, signed "Glasfabrik, Karlsbad." Decanter is 16" high, c. 1890.

Plate 11 Flower-form vase with gilded foliate decoration; Moser. Height 14", c. 1885.

Plate 12 Animal and fish-form vases were popular during the 1880s. Items decorated in the style shown are generally attributed to Moser; however, this has not been confirmed. Cat is 7¼" high. Pokal, collection of Mr. Ronald Pugliese.

Plate 13 Enameled fern-leaf patterns were popular Moser decorative themes; Moser. Height 6", c. 1885. Collection of Mr. Ronald Pugliese.

Plate 14 Tooled rims of the type illustrated have, to date, only been found on Moser decorated glass; Moser. Plate is 5³/₄" in diameter, c. 1885.

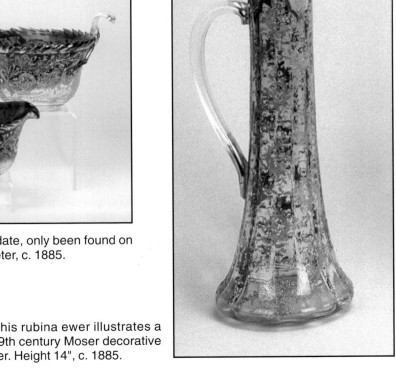

Plate 15 This rubina ewer illustrates a classical 19th century Moser decorative motif; Moser. Height 14", c. 1885.

Plate 16 Fern-leaf decorated glassware is available in many different variants; Moser. Pitcher is 5½" high, c. 1885.

Plate 17 Brass mounts on Moser caskets appear to be of unique design and were probably manufactured at Meistersdorf; Moser. Height 4½", c. 1885.

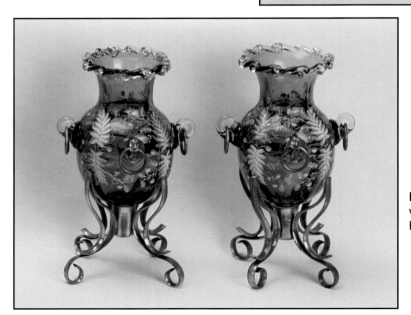

Plate 18 Mounted fern-leaf decorated vases are not commonly found; Moser. Height 8", c. 1885.

Plate 19 Islamic design influences are evident in this popular decorative motif; Moser. Vase is 4" high, c. 1885.

Plate 20 Large jewels in intricate enameled settings represent a standard Moser decorative form; Moser. Height 4$\frac{1}{8}$", c. 1885.

Plate 21 Islamic inspired decorative motifs were popular in the 1880s; Moser. Decanter on the right is 9$\frac{1}{2}$" high. Circa 1885.

Plate 22 Intricate geometric patterns are characteristic of Islamic designs. Attributed to Moser. Charger is 14" in diameter, c. 1885.

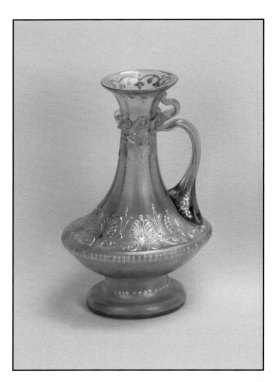

Plate 23 Iridescent finish, Islamic form and characteristic Moser decorative patterns are combined in this example. Attributed to Moser. Height 6$\frac{7}{8}$", c. 1885.

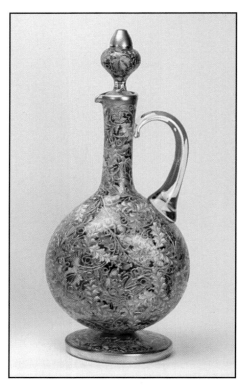

Plate 24 Combining enameled foliate patterns with stylized flowers was a typical Moser characteristic. Attributed to Moser. Height 12$\frac{3}{4}$", c. 1885.

Plate 25 Unique multicolored flower-form vase with Islamic style decoration. Attributed to Moser. Height 9$\frac{5}{8}$", c. 1885.

Plate 26 Fused molded glass forms combined with oven-work and enameling was a popular Moser artistic form; Moser. Height 6¹/₈", c. 1885.

Plate 27 Enameled flower-form vases occur in multiple shapes and sizes; Moser. Vase on the right is 10⁵/₈" high, c. 1885.

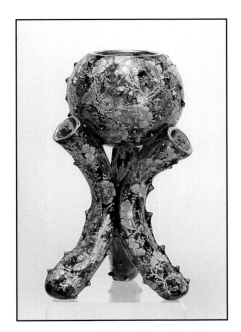

Plate 28 This tri-footed rose bowl was a difficult glass form to produce; Moser. Height 9¹/₄", c. 1885.

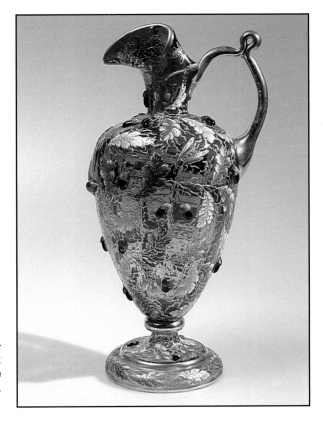

Plate 29 Applied glass acorns with brightly enameled oak leaves is a classical Moser artistic form; Moser. Height 14", c. 1885. Collection of the Chrysler Museum of Art, #71.6610. Gift of Walter P. Chrysler, Jr.

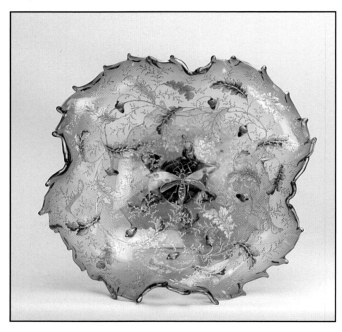

Plate 30 Naturalistic decorative elements and forms were typical of Moser production (side view); Moser. Height 6½", c. 1885.

Plate 31 Top view of tazza in Plate 30.

Plate 32 Decorative motifs relating to wine dominated Central European artistic glass; Moser. Height 11⅛", c. 1885.

Plate 33 Variegated lemon-yellow glass was primarily produced in Bohemia. Attributed to Moser. Height 14", c. 1885.

Plate 34 Typical of Victorian glass forms, this tour-de-force was probably intended for the English market (top view); Moser. 15½" in diameter, c. 1885. Collection of Mr. Ronald Pugliese.

Plate 35 Side view of the bowl in Plate 34. Height 9".

Plate 36 Amberina pitcher with sculptured bird and grape clusters; Moser. Height 6¹⁄₈", c. 1885.

Plate 37 Gilded and platinated beaker decorated with coat-of-arms and oak leaves. Attributed to Moser. Height 9¹⁄₂", c. 1885.

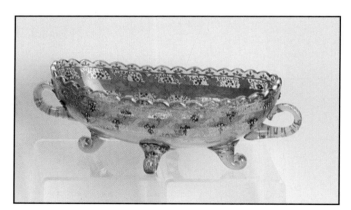

Plate 38 Grape clusters were generally simulated with applied glass beading; Moser. Bowl is 10³⁄₈" long by 3¹⁄₄" high, c. 1885.

Plate 39 Traditional Bohemian hunting mug. Attributed to Moser. Height 6¹⁄₄", c. 1885.

Plate 40 Applied acorns and oak leaves were applied to a wide variety of glass colors and forms; Moser. Height 6", c. 1885.

Plate 41 Heavily enameled loving cup inscribed in English "Good Health, My Friend, Every Time"; Moser. Height 7½", c. 1885.

Plate 42 Applied salamanders and enameled fish on stained crackle-glass reflect Moser's emphasis on naturalistic aquatic life forms. Attributed to Moser. Vases on the left, c. 1885, are 9⅛" high; pitcher on the right is c. 1920.

Plate 43 Simulated naturalistic settings, combined with insect and animal glass forms, were a specialty of Moser decorators; Moser. Vase (top, left) is 8¼" high. Circa 1880–90.

Plate 44 Birds sculptured in enamel represent a highly sought-after Moser decorative technique; Moser. Height 5⅝", c. 1885.

Plate 45 Artistic balance and grace are evident in this exceptional sculptured eagle vase; Moser. Height 14", c. 1885.

Plate 46 Mold-blown glass combined with enameled floral decoration is an unusual Moser form. Signed "Moser." Height 8⅝", c. 1880–1920.

Plate 47 An exceptional pair of deep amethyst colored vases with sculptured Rococo scrollwork. Attributed to Moser. Height 15", c. 1880–90.

Plate 48 Stained amber crackle-glass Bohemian crystal glassware with aquatic life forms was produced by Moser. Pitcher on left is 4⅞" high. Circa 1900–1925.

Plate 49 Heavily jeweled vase, probably made for the Russian market. Attributed to Moser. Height 8¼", c. 1885.

Plate 50 Intaglio-cut glassware with floral bouquets was produced in considerable quantities by Moser. Center bottle is signed "Moser, Karlsbad." Vase on the left is 7³/₄" high, c. 1880–1920.

Plate 51 Intaglio-cut flowers and birds were a favorite subject matter for Moser engravers. Attributed to Moser. Dish is 14" in diameter. Circa 1880–1920.

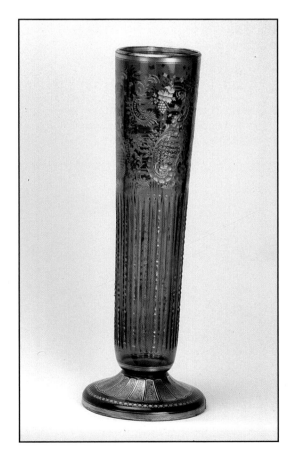

Plate 52 Lavender glass of this color is quite rare. Attributed to Moser. Height 11⁵/₈", c. 1880–1920.

Plate 53 Finely detailed gold filigree vase with floral engraved cabochons. Attributed to Moser. Height 7¼", c. 1885.

Plate 54 Cordials with underplates are difficult to find; Moser. Underplate is 3⅝" in diameter, c. 1885.

Plate 55 This vase exemplifies the universal appeal of Moser decorative motifs; Moser. Height 7¼", c. 1885.

Plate 56 Floral enameling on a gilded ground was apparently quite popular and produced over a considerable time period; Moser. Pokal is 13" high, c. 1880–1930.

Plate 57 Vermicular enameling and stylized insects and flowers appear to be offshoots of Moser's adaptation of Japanese Kakaimon decorative forms; Moser. Vase in the center is 5³/₄" high. Circa 1885.

Plate 58 Dense gilded patterns reflect Islamic design influences; Moser. Vase is signed "Moser,." 7¹/₂" high, c. 1885.

Plate 59 Intricate gold and platinum decoration on a classical Pokal form is singularly striking in appearance. Attributed to Moser. Height 23¹/₈", c. 1885.

Plate 60 Composite enamel-gilt and gilded engraving were combined with raised colored cabochons. Cup and saucer are signed "Moser." Decanter is 8³/₄" high. Circa 1885.

Plate 61 Two styles of decorative enamel found on Moser cabochon decorated glassware; Moser. Chalice on the right is 8¹/₄" high. Circa 1885.

Plate 62 Sugar shakers of this form are rare; Moser. Height 5³/₄", c. 1885.

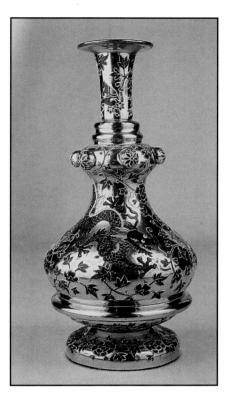

Plate 63 Coralene enhanced enameled flowers combined with Mary Gregory type enameling was a popular decorative motif. Attributed to Moser. Vase (right) is 11¹⁄₈" high. Circa 1890–1925.

Plate 64 Original Moser adaptation of the Japanese Kakaimon Rock Blossom motif, c. 1885.

Plate 65 Mary Gregory style vase marketed by Moser. Vase retains its original paper label. Height 11³⁄₈", c. 1885.

Plate 66 Japanese derived decorative motifs can be found in a variety of styles; Moser. Obelisk is 8⁵⁄₈" high. Circa 1885.

Plate 67 Lead crystal water set produced by St.-Louis and decorated by Moser. Signed "Moser, Karlsbad." Pitcher is 9$\frac{1}{2}$" high. Circa 1885.

Plate 68 Second generation Moser adaptation of Japanese Kakaimon Rock Blossom motif; Moser. Bowl is 9$\frac{1}{2}$" in diameter. Circa 1885.

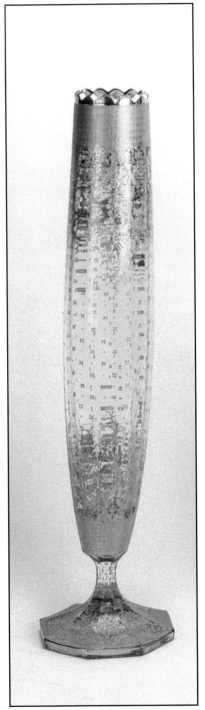

Plate 69 Multiple gold and enamel decorative techniques were combined to decorate this vase; Moser. Height 21$\frac{5}{8}$".

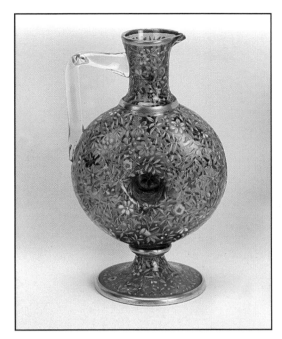

Plate 70 Donut-shaped decanters and ewers are an unusual form. Attributed to Moser. Height 9", c. 1885.

Plate 71 Rose bowls were a popular form during the Victorian period; Moser. Small bowl has a paper label of an unidentified Vienna marketing firm, marked "Karlsbad-Vienna." Large bowls are 7" high, c. 1885.

Plate 72 Complete dinner services of this period are difficult to find. Moser. Decanter is 10¼" high. Circa 1885. Collection of Dr. and Mrs. Darryl McLeod.

Plate 73 Dense composite enamel-gilt foliate decorative patterns, such as this, were produced in large quantities; Moser. Decanter is 7³/₄" high. Circa 1885.

Plate 74 German neo-Renaissance glassware produced by Moser is difficult to identify. Attributed to Moser. Salt is 2³/₄" high. Circa 1885.

Plate 75 Miniatures were sometimes purely decorative or could have been salesman samples. Moser, c. 1885.

Plate 76 Tumble-ups, complete with underplates, are rare; Moser. Height 8¼", c. 1885.

Plate 77 Water pitchers, such as this, would complement any table setting. Attributed to Moser. Height 8", c. 1885.

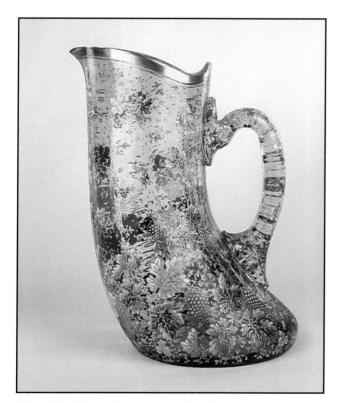

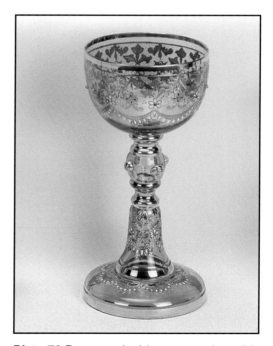

Plate 78 Pitcher decorated in classical Moser grape pattern. Rubina Verde blank with enameled, rather than applied, glass grapes probably dates this example after 1895; Moser. Height 9¼".

Plate 79 Decorated tableware, such as this large water goblet, was available in a variety of sizes; Moser. Height 8⅜", c. 1885.

Plate 80 These decanter sets display a popular Moser decorative pattern; Moser. Decanter on the left is 10½" high. Circa 1885.

Plate 81 High density decorative patterns seem to have a life of their own. Attributed to Moser. Vases are 10¾" high. Circa 1885.

Plate 82 Glass humidors are rare. Attributed to Moser. Height 9¾", c. 1885.

Plate 83 Wide gilded rim bands were often employed by Moser decorators. Moser. height 16³/₄", c. 1885.

Plate 84 Decanter set in unusual gilded multicolored pattern; tray is 12¹/₄" in diameter. Attributed to Moser, c. 1885.

Plate 85 Dome topped boxes were apparently popular items in the 19th century. Moser. Box on upper right is 3³/₄" high. Circa 1885.

Plate 86 Floral enameling on a stained red ground. Attributed to Moser. Vases are 7¹/₂" high, c. 1885.

Plate 87 Fired gold leaf, used as an engraving filler, left indistinct boundaries. Attributed to Moser. Height 9", c. 1885.

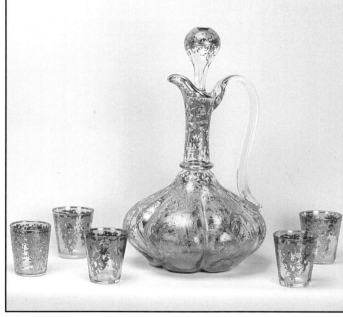

Plate 88 Lavender enamel on blue glass is an unusual but pleasing combination. Attributed to Moser. Decanter is 9" high, c. 1885.

Plate 89 Elegant gilded patterns combined with complimentary glass forms distinguish Moser production; Moser. Decanter is 10³/₈" high. Circa 1885.

Plate 90 Iridescent Bohemian crystal enhances the appearance of delicately enameled glassware; Moser. Height 4³/₄", c. 1885.

Plate 91 Heavy platinum and gold produces striking decorative effects. Attributed to Moser. Height 5⁷/₈", c. 1885.

Plate 92 An interesting combination of cutting, engraving, gilding and enameling techniques; Moser. Height 5¹/₄", c. 1885.

Plate 93 Subtle decorative forms, which depart from the mainstream of Moser production, can be found. Vases, center and right, are signed "Moser." The center vase is 6³/₄" high. Circa 1880–1900.

Plate 94 Distinctive patterns, such as these, aid dramatically in identifying Moser glassware; Moser. Römers are 4" high, c. 1885.

Plate 95 Acanthus scrollwork patterns were employed over four decades; Moser. Footed plate on the left is 6³/₄" in diameter, c. 1885. The other plate and goblet are c. 1930.

Plate 96 Decanter set in the French Empire style was probably produced for the French market. Signed "Moser." Decanter is 8⁵/₈" high, c. 1885.

Plate 97 Acanthus scrollwork combined with a characteristic Moser vermicular pattern; Moser. Height 12$^{1}/_{8}$", c. 1885.

Plate 98 Pokal displaying a distinctive brightly enameled Moser decorative motif; Moser. Height 16$^{1}/_{4}$", c. 1885.

Plate 99 Temperature colored amberina produced in Bohemia was distinctively different than its American counterpart. Center vase is signed "Moser." Vase on the left is 9⅞" high. Circa 1880–1900 est.

Plate 100 Cased Bohemian amberina colored glassware is difficult to distinguish from American versions. Attributed to Moser. Height 9⅝". Circa 1880–1900 est.

Plate 101 Transparent enamels add a new dimension to gilded decorative motifs; Moser. Flask is 10" long. Circa 1880–1910.

Plate 102 Modernized versions of the cased cabochon glassware pictured in Plate 60. Attributed to Moser. Pitcher is 11" high, circa 1910–1930 est.

Plate 103 High-relief floral decoration was produced by Moser as early as the Art Nouveau period. Attributed to Moser. Height 16", c. 1890–1910.

Plate 104 Selected Moser wine goblets showing the wide diversity of styles available, c. 1880–1930.

Plate 105 Selected Moser wine goblets, c. 1880–1930.

Plate 106 Moser juice glasses illustrating the wide selection of decorative patterns available, c. 1880–1930.

Plate 107 Selected Moser juice glasses, c. 1880–1930.

Plate 108 After 1890, decorative patterns complemented, rather than dominated, glass forms; Moser. Height 5¹/₂", c. 1890–1914.

Plate 109 Abbreviated decorative motifs were produced after approximately 1890; Moser. Decanter is 13¹/₂" high, c. 1890–1914.

Plate 110 Although Moser's decorative patterns became less complex, basic compositional characteristics were largely retained. Center vase is signed "Glasfabrik, Karlsbad." Vase on the right is 9¹/₂" high. Circa 1890–1920.

Plate 111 Rubina Verde shaded glassware of this coloration was probably produced at Meierhöfen; Moser. Vase on the left is signed "Moser" and is 12¼" high. Circa 1895–1930.

Plate 112 Baroque Graffito scrollwork, enameled garlands and figural groupings were distinctive Bohemian decorative motifs. Venetian blank signed in enamel "Murano"; decoration attributed to Moser. Charger is 14⅝" in diameter, c. 1900.

Plate 113 Venetian style decoration on a distinctive Moser facet-cut blank; Moser. Height 6⅞", c. 1910–30.

Plate 114 Venetian style glass-ware, decorated as shown, was probably sold outside of Italy. Plate is Venetian glass, signed "Moser" and is 8" in diameter. Sugar and creamer may have been totally produced in Bohemia. Moser, c. 1900.

Plate 115 A 16th century Spanish canine and foliate pattern used by Moser decorators. Salviati glass blank on the left; Central European glass blank on the right. Moser enameling. Underplate is 7$^1/_2$". Circa 1900.

Plate 116 Decorative glassware of this type was marketed by Salviati under their own name. Cup and saucer in the center are signed "Moser." Goblet is 6$^3/_8$" high. Circa 1900–1910.

Plate 117 Jewish ceremonial goblets of this type were probably produced by Moser using Venetian glass blanks. The Goblet on the left is 7⁷⁄₈" high, c. 1890–1910.

Plate 118 Baroque gold Graffito applied to Central European glass blanks. Attributed to Moser. Decanter is 11³⁄₈" high. Circa 1900–1910.

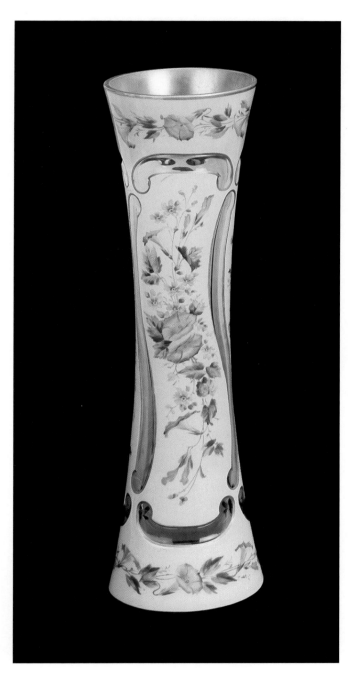

Plate 119 Enameled flowers on cased opaque white glass was a popular European decorative motif. Signed "Glasfabrik, Karlsbad." Height 15³⁄₄", c. 1900–1920.

Plate 120 Moser Art Nouveau engraved glassware was of the highest quality. Height 8⁵/₈", c. 1900–10.

Plate 121 Moser engraved Art Nouveau glassware reflects a graceful and elegant style. Height 13¹/₂", c. 1900–10.

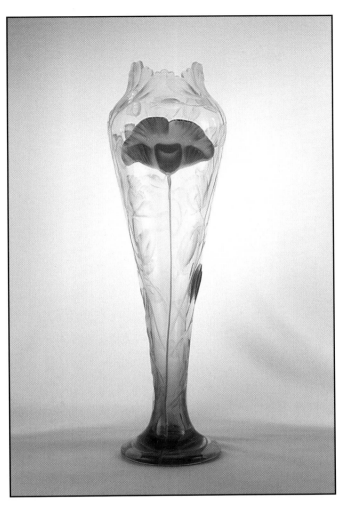

Plate 122 By combining multiple two-layer cased marquetry cameo-cut insets, a trailing marquetry stem, a shaded glass blank, floral relief cutting around the rim and intaglio body engraving, this example reflects a composite of Moser engraved Art Nouveau glassware decorative motifs. Signed "Moser, Karlsbad." Height 18", c. 1900–10.

Plate 123 Double shaded marquetry decorated glassware required considerable skill to produce. Signed "Moser, Karlsbad." Height 6¹⁄₂", c. 1900–10.

Plate 124 Marquetry wine goblets would complement the finest table services; Moser. The left goblet is 8" high. Circa 1900–10.

Plate 125 Moser's "Paolo" or "Rose" pattern has been in continuous production since 1900. This colored example probably predates 1930. Decanter is 14" high.

Plate 126 Marquetry insets were occasionally of multilayer cased construction; Moser. Height 4³/₄", c. 1900–10.

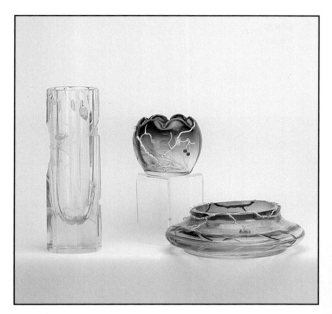

Plate 127 Glass and enameled accents, such as berries, insects and vines were occasionally applied to engraved Art Nouveau glassware; Moser. Vase at left is 7" high. Circa 1900–10.

Plate 129 Three-handled vase has three distinctively different engraved floral motifs; Moser. Height 6⁷/₈", c. 1900–10.

Plate 128 Moser engraved Art Nouveau was available in a wide range of shapes and sizes. Vase at right is 7¹/₂" high. Circa 1900–10.

Plate 130 Moser engraved cruet with unusual facet-cut stopper (stoppers of engraved Art Nouveau glassware were generally also engraved); Moser. Height 7³/₄", c. 1900–10.

Plate 131 Blue and Yellow colored examples of Moser engraved Art Nouveau glassware are quite rare. Atomizer on the left is signed "Moser Karlsbad." Atomizer in the center is 6" high. Circa 1900–1910.

Plate 132 An interesting comparison between Moser (left) and Harrach (right) Art Nouveau glassware. The Moser vase is 9⁵/₈" high, c. 1900–10.

Plate 133 Moser produced limited quantities of acid-cut cameo comparable to the best work produced in France. Signed in cameo "Moser Karlsbad." Height 6¹/₈", c. 1900–14.

Plate 134 The majority of Moser acid-cut cameo was produced on two color blanks. Signed "Moser Karlsbad." Height 3¹/₂", c. 1900–14.

Plate 135 Karlsbader Secession glass was only produced for a limited time. Signed "Moser Karlsbad." Height 19", c. 1900–10.

Plate 136 Art Nouveau period floral motifs were employed for a considerable time after their inception; Moser. Decanter is 14⅝" high. Circa 1910–20.

Plate 137 Moser cut glass was generally accented with enameled decoration. Bowl (center) is signed "Moser, Karlsbad, Austria." Pitcher at right is 10¾" high. Circa 1910–25.

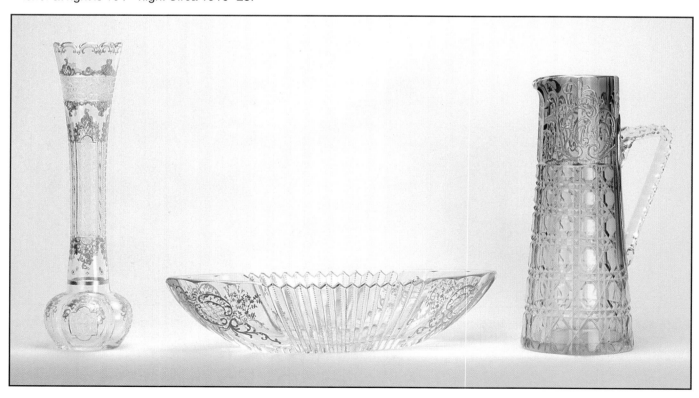

Plate 138 Grouping of vases which illustrate the "large floral enameling" motif. Second vase from left is signed "Moser" and has its original paper label. The vase on the right is signed "Moser." The vase at left is 14⅝" high. Circa 1910–25.

Plate 139 Applied bees became an important decorative motif after approximately 1900. Vase at right is signed "Moser." Vase at left is 14⅝" high. Circa 1910–25.

Plate 140 Amazon warrior cameo-frieze decoration was designed by Leo Moser in 1914; dark green glass. Signed "Made in Czecho Slovakia, Moser, Karlsbad." Height 17", c. 1918–22

Plate 141 A particularly beautiful adaptation of Moser floral enameling. Attributed to Moser. Vase at left is 8" high. Circa 1910–25.

Plate 142 Shaded blanks were rarely used with frieze decoration. Signed "Made in Czecho Slovakia, Moser, Karlsbad." Decanter is 8³/₄" high. Circa 1918–22.

Plate 143 Cameo patterns employed by Moser were finely executed; Radion glass. Signed "Made in Czecho Slovakia, Moser, Karlsbad." Height 11³/₄", circa 1918–22.

Plate 144 Moser cameo-friezes were applied to a wide variety of glass forms. Signed "Czecho Slovakia, Moser, Karlsbad." Height 4¹/₂", c. 1918–22.

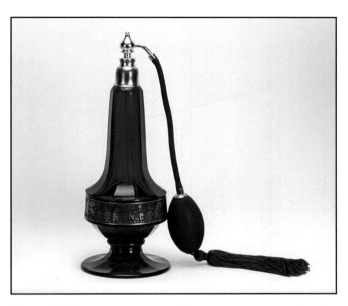

Plate 145 Moser cameo atomizers were apparently quite popular; Moser. Height 8⁷/₈", c. 1918–25.

Plate 146 Scenic vases of this type are unusual; enameled decoration applied to an acid textured crystal blank. Signed "Moser Karlsbad," "MK" and with an artist's cipher. Height 19³/₁₆", c. 1920. Collection of the Chrysler Museum of Art, #71.6612. Gift of Walter P. Chrysler, Jr.

Plate 147 After 1922, the production of Moser enameled glassware was apparently moved to the Meyr's Neffe glassworks; Moser. Chalices are 12¹/₂" high. Circa 1925.

Plate 148 Moser's "Royal" pattern was produced for a considerable time period; Moser. Decanter is 10⅞" high. Circa 1925.

Plate 149 Heavily jeweled glassware, such as this beer pitcher and glasses, continued to be produced after World War I. Attributed to Moser. Pitcher is 18" high. Circa 1925 est.

Plate 150 This jeweled vase displays a decorative pattern which was apparently quite popular with Moser enamelists. Attributed to Moser. Height 8⅝", c. 1925 est.

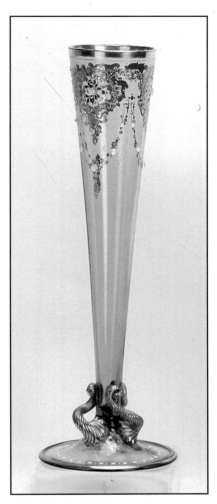

Plate 151 Twisted base supports add interest to an otherwise common form. Attributed to Moser. Height 12", c. 1925 est.

Plate 152 Engraved lidded bowl with unusual blue over brown over clear casing. Signed "Moser, Karlsbad." Height (with lid) 6⅞", c. 1918–25 est.

Plate 153 Probably produced at Meyr's Neffe glassworks, this jeweled tumbler is signed "Lobmeyr," c. 1925.

Plate 155 Wedding goblets, such as this, were designed for drinking from either end. Attributed to Moser. Height 8⁷/₈", c. 1910–30.

Plate 154 High-relief floral decoration was primarily produced during the 1920s and 1930s, but had probable origins prior to 1890. Attributed to Moser. Height 13", c. 1910–30.

Plate 156 Designed by Stephan Rath after an original in the Prague Museum. Part of Lobmeyer table set #253 (still in production). Signed "Moser" and "Lobmeyr." Height 7³/₄", c. 1925.

Plate 157 Enamel decoration reminiscent of 19th c. forms but produced after 1918. This example bears its original paper label and is signed "Moser." Height 9¼", c. 1918–30.

Plate 158 Classic Bohemian Pokal form with gold colored decoration; Moser. Height 11⅞", circa 1925.

Plate 159 Moser's "Animor" series was apparently commercially quite successful. *Left,* signed in cameo, "Moser Karlsbad" and "MK," height 11¾". *Right,* signed in cameo "MK." Circa 1925.

Plate 160 Moser's "Masque" series was only produced for a limited time period. Signed in cameo, "Moser Karlsbad." Height 15⅛", c. 1925.

Plate 162 Moser rainbow colored glass, produced at Meierhöfen, can be easily mistaken for glassware produced by other glasshouses. Moser, c. 1895–1925.

Plate 161 Cameo stork patterns are fairly rare. Signed "Moser Karlsbad, Czecho Slovakia." Height 10¼", c. 1920.

Plate 164 Characteristic Chris Lebeau shallow bowl produced at Meierhöfen. 11½" diameter, c. 1925.

Plate 163 Engraved wine goblet with classic Lobmeyr design. Probably produced at the Meyr's Neffe glassworks. Moser, c. 1925.

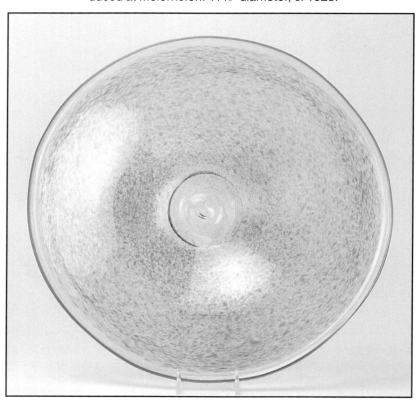

Plate 165 Cased and facet-cut Art Deco glassware of unusual form. Both examples signed "Moser." Vase at left is 7½" high, c. 1930 est. Examples of this type were produced after World War II.

Plate 166 Diamond point "stipple" engraving was first introduced by the Dutch. Signed with artist's monogram and "Moser." Height 6¼", c. 1925.

Plate 167 Fanciful chargers probably produced for the Spanish market; Moser. Signed "Royo." 11½" diameter, c. 1925.

Plate 168 Heinrich Haussman deep acid cut-back decorative glassware. Signed "Moser." Vase is 6³/₄" high. Circa 1928–30.

Plate 169 Rare-earth colored glasses brought Moser international recognition. *Left to right:* 7³/₄" high, signed "Moser Karlsbad-Royalit," c. 1922–25; signed "Moser Karlsbad-Heliolit," c. 1922–25; Royalit, unsigned, c. 1922–30.

Plate 169b Occasionally, portions of sets became damaged and had to be replaced by the Moser factory. This set, produced in Royalit, retains its original cordials and stopper. The decanter, however, is a near Royalit facsimile. Signed "Moser." Decanter is 9¹/₄" high. Circa 1930.

Plate 170 Alexandrit was the most popular rare-earth glass produced by Moser. All pieces are signed "Moser." Vase at top left is 7⅝" high. Circa 1925–30.

Plate 171 Moser's "Splendid" dinnerware service is still in production.

Plate 172 Moser Heliolit is brown under tungsten light and green under fluorescent light. All pieces are signed "Moser Karlsbad-Heliolit." Vase is 14¾" high. Circa 1922–25.

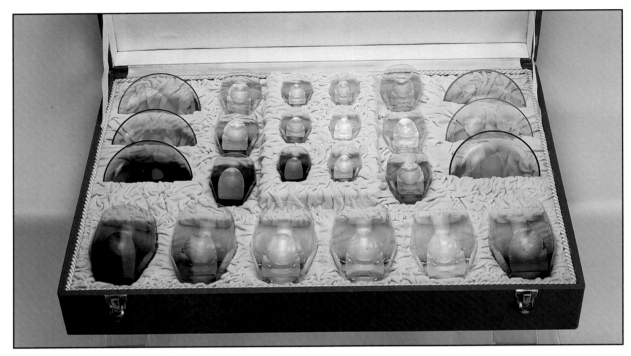

Plate 173 Glass colors developed by Moser won international acclaim. Pattern is designated "ice bottom." *Colors from left to right:* Smoke, Topaz, Beryl, Alexandrit, Eldor and Rosa. Each piece is signed "Moser," c. 1925.

Plate 174 Moser's Eldor is one of the most beautiful glass colors ever produced. Signed "Moser." Decanter is 10¼" high. Circa 1920–30.

Plate 175 This Art Deco cutting style was extensively produced by Moser. Both examples are signed "Moser." Decanter on the left is 10⅜" high. Circa 1925.

Plate 176 Art Deco dresser sets and accessories, cut in this cubistic pattern, were widely produced. Signed "Moser, Karlovy Vary-Made in Czechoslovakia." Atomizer is 5¼" high. Circa 1930.

Plate 177 Moser glassware was available in presentation sets with or without engraved decoration. Box is signed "Bohemia, Moser, Praha," c. 1925.

Plate 178 Decanter cut in another popular Art Deco cutting style. Signed "Moser." Height 18", c. 1925.

Plate 178b Multiple Art Deco cutting styles were produced by Moser. *Left to right:* Unsigned, 5³/₄" high; unsigned; signed "Moser"; signed "Moser"; signed "Moser, Karlovy Vary-Made in Czecho-slovakia." Circa 1930.

Plate 179 Moser developed glass types exclusively for use by the Wiener Werkstätte. Signed "WW Moser," c. 1925. Collection of the Prague Museum of Decorative Arts.

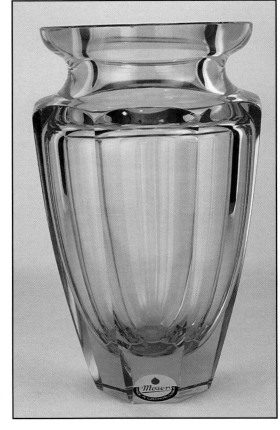

Plate 180 Moser Beryl Iris Vase. Height 8¹/₂", c. 1975. Collection of Tradewinds Furniture & Crystal.

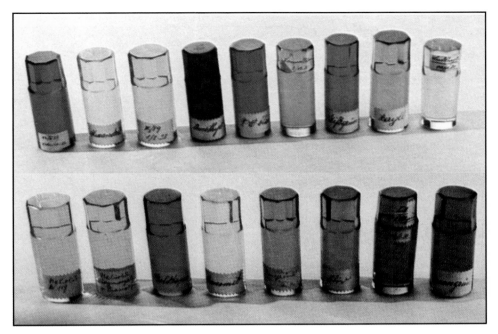

Plate 181 Non rare-earth Moser glass color samples, c. 1920–30. Collection of Mr. and Mrs. Harry Foreman.

Plate 182 Moser Bikava facet-cut vase with cameo band of Amazon warriors. Modern Fantazie Moser with cameo friezes of the type illustrated are referred to by the name "Sovereign." Height 5¾", c. 1975. Collection of Tradewinds Furniture & Crystal.

Plate 183 Moser Bikava Corset vase. Height 10¼", c. 1975. Collection of Tradewinds Furniture & Crystal.

Plate 184 Moser Beryl "Sovereign" Vase. Height 9⅛", c. 1975. Collection of Tradewinds Furniture & Crystal.

Plate 185 Moser cobalt blue "Sovereign" vase. Height 6³/₈",
c. 1975. Collection of Tradewinds Furniture & Crystal.

Plate 186 Moser "Rosalin" Pedestal vase. Height 11¹/₈",
c. 1975. Collection of Tradewinds Furniture & Crystal.

Plate 187 Moser Eldor facet-cut vase. Height 7³/₄", c.
1975. Collection of Tradewinds Furniture & Crystal.

Plate 188 Moser Royalit "Sovereign" vase. Height 6", c.
1975. Collection of Tradewinds Furniture & Crystal.

Plate 189 This engraved "Alexandrit" decanter was produced after 1945. Signed "Moser." Height 18³/₄".

Plate 191 Moser facet-cut Hock wine goblets, c. 1975. Collection of Tradewinds Furniture & Crystal.

Plate 190 Moser facet-cut "Rosalin" Tulip vase. Height 8³/₈", c. 1975. Collection of Tradewinds Furniture & Crystal.

Plate 192 Moser facet-cut "Rosalin" rose bowl. Height 6³/₈", c. 1975. Collection of Tradewinds Furniture & Crystal.

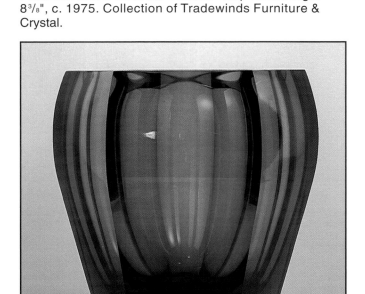

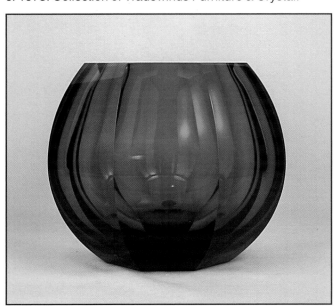

Plate 193 Moser engraved Hock wine goblets, c. 1975. Collection of Tradewinds Furniture & Crystal.

Plate 194 Moser Amethyst "Sovereign" facet-cut vase. Height 9½", c. 1975. Collection of Tradewinds Furniture & Crystal.

Plate 195 Moser facet-cut Hock wine with shallow gilded cameo band, c. 1975. Collection of Tradewinds Furniture & Crystal.

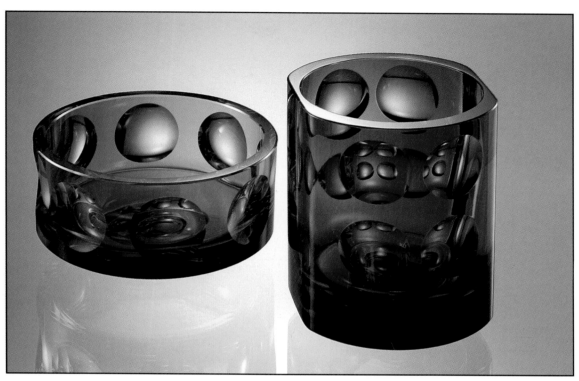

Plate 196 Adolf Matura. Vase and bowl with lens cutting (prod. nos. 2158, 2159). Designed in 1974. 8½"
and 9" in diameter.

Plate 197 Jiří Šuhájek. Cut vase (prod. no. 2238). Designed in 1975.
Height 7".

Plate 198 Vienna Modern cutting styles formed a foundation for Moser decorative efforts. Unknown maker, c. 1925.

Plate 199 Meyr's Neffe's and Moser's decorative styles closely paralleled each other. Goblet was produced by Meyr's Neffe; the cup and saucer are signed "Moser." Circa 1885.

Plate 200 Similarity in decorative styles is quite evident in this comparison. Shallow bowl is signed "Lobmeyr" and was probably produced by Meyr's Neffe. Cup and saucer are signed "Moser." Circa 1885.

Plate 201 Attributed to Moser by Cox, this type of decoration was either performed by Moser or Meyr's Neffe (or both) decorators. Height 13", c. 1885.

Plate 202 Pokal decorated in Schwartzlot Chinoiserie pattern typical of Ignaz Preissler. Produced by Meyr's Neffe. Height 20½", c. 1885.

Plate 203 Exquisite workmanship—Moser or Meyr's Neffe? Height 4¼", c. 1885.

Plate 204 Acanthus scrollwork and fish scale decoration is normally attributed to Meyr's Neffe; however, this pattern was also produced by Graff Harrach. Unsigned. Decanter is from Lobmeyr's no. 81 table service and is 10" high. Circa 1885.

Plate 205 Finger bowls were popular additions to table services. *From left to right:* cased cranberry acid-etched cameo bowl with Fostoria decorative pattern, unsigned; ruby glass bowl with gold Baroque Graffito decoration, signed "Venice & Murano Glass Co." Circa 1900.

Plate 206 Acid-etched wine goblets in lead crystal. Attributed to St.-Louis, c. 1900.

Plate 207 Baroque acid cut-back cameo table-ware in lead crystal. Signed "Moser"; glass attributed to St.-Louis, c. 1900.

Plate 208 Malachite vases of this form were produced in Bohemia prior to World War I. Height 8⅝".

Plate 209 Webb enameled glassware employed patterns similar to those used by Moser decorators. Thomas Webb & Sons (England). Vase on the right is 10½" high. Circa 1880–90.

Plate 210 Webb vases enameled in a typical Moser style. Center vase is 10" high. Circa 1885.

Plate 211 Webb rainbow glass is easily mistaken for Moser; Thomas Webb & Sons. Vase on the left is 6³/₄" high. Circa 1900–20 est.

Plate 212 Harrach typically employed gold highlights in their engraved Art Nouveau glassware, c. 1900.

Plate 213 Art Nouveau style enameling with multicolored marquetry inset; Graff Harrach. Height 10", c. 1890.

Plate 214 Harrach specialized in multicolored marquetry decoration; Graff Harrach. Height 9⁷/₈", c. 1900.

Plate 215 Comparison of Harrach (center) and Moser (right and left) engraved Art Nouveau glassware, c. 1900.

Plate 216 Heavy gold enamel scrollwork is similar to Moser decorative forms; Graff Harrach. Height 11", c. 1860. Collection of Robert and Deborah Truitt.

Plate 217 Harrach cased vase with multicolored enamel and gold decoration. Height 4½", c. 1895. Collection of Robert and Deborah Truitt.

Plate 218 Applied precast decorative objects were employed by Harrach and Moser decorators alike; Graff Harrach. Height 9⅜", c. 1900.

Plate 219 Applied beading, combined with enamel and gold, were primary design elements employed by Moser decorators; Fritz Heckert. Height 7", c. 1890. Collection of Robert and Deborah Truitt.

Plate 220 Cobalt blue glass, visually identical to the Moser glass in Plate 145, with a finely detailed cameo frieze. Produced by A. R. (Adolf Rosche?), Haida, c. 1920. Height 4⅞".

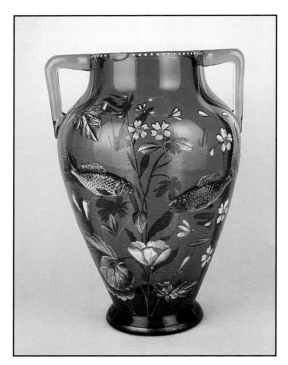

Plate 221 Enameled vase with applied glass fish; glass composition is identical to that of the Moser vase in Plate 139. Decoration attributed to Harrach, c. 1890–1910. Height 10¼".

Plate 222 Transparent enameled panels outlined with gilded engraving is a dominant design characteristic employed by Heckert decorators. Height 11⅜", c. 1885.

Plate 223 Like Moser, Heckert employed flowers, birds and insects in their decorative designs. Signed "Fritz Heckert." Height 12⁵⁄₈", c. 1885.

Plate 224 Wine goblets strongly resembling Moser decorated glassware. Signed "Fritz Heckert." *Left,* c. 1910–25; *right,* c. 1885.

Plate 225 Heckert produced jeweled, gilded and cut glassware easily mistaken for Moser. Signed "Fritz Heckert." Chalice is 8⁷⁄₈" high. Circa 1910–30.

Plate 226 Josephinenhütte ewer decorated in gold and platinum. Signed. Height 15¹⁄₂", c. 1885.

Plate 227 Josephinenhütte iridescent loving cup decorated in the Islamic style. Height 5⅝", c. 1885.

Plate 228 Delicately enamel-gilt decorated tableware. Signed "Josephinenhütte," c. 1890–1920.

Plate 229 Rössler "Color Cake" decorated glassware. Height 3⅛", c. 1920–30.

Plate 230 Riedel decorated glassware. Center vase is cased blue over opaque-white glass, c. 1893. Tall goblets are coralene over enamel, 16¾" high, c. 1880, and were probably enameled in Vinzenz Pohl's workshop.

Plate 231 Riedel tankard with Schwartzlot decoration. Height 3⅝", c. 1890.

Plate 232 Löetz "Agate" enameled vase. Height 4½", c. 1890. Collection of Robert and Deborah Truitt.

Plate 233 Löetz enameled iridescent vase in gilded brass mounts. Height 8¼", c. 1895.

Plate 234 Löetz "Carneal" rigaree footed vase with Moser type rim enameling. Height 5", c. 1890. Collection of Robert and Deborah Truitt.

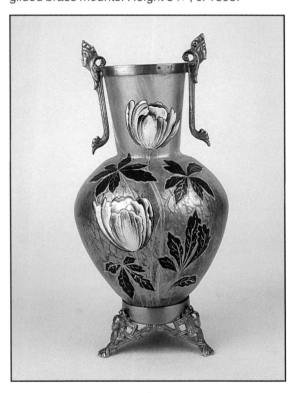

Plate 235 Löetz threaded iridescent glassware with enameled floral decoration. Vase is 11 1/2" high, c. 1900–20.

Plate 236 Facet-cut Pedestal vase. Attributed to Goldberg. Height 6 3/8", c. 1925.

Plate 237 Emerald green facet-cut lidded container. Signed "Made in Czecho-Slovakia." Height 6 1/4", c. 1925.

Plate 238 Brocard decorated cordial goblet, c. 1880–90.

Plate 239 Cameo-cut and enameled vase. Signed with a Bishop's head surrounded by "Mont Joye" and "L & C" (Legras & Cie). Height 28", c. 1900. Collection of the Chrysler Museum of Art, #71.7703A. Gift of Walter P. Chrysler, Jr.

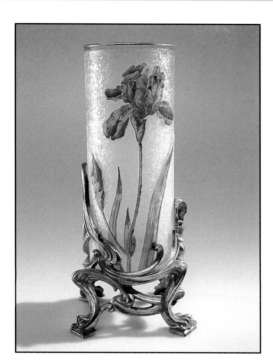

Plate 240 Mont Joye (Legras & Cie) enameled iris on acid cut-back crystal; gilded Art Nouveau brass base. Unsigned. Height 12", c. 1910. Collection of the Chrysler Museum of Art, #77.1290. Gift of Walter P. Chrysler, Jr.

Plate 241 Although stylized in form, floral enameling of this type is quite easily attributed to Moser. Signed "Sèvres." Height 7", c. 1900.

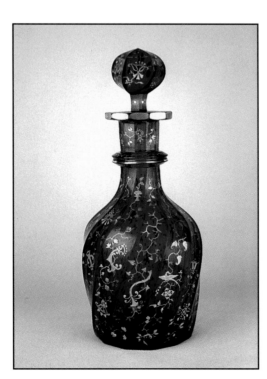

Plate 242 Well preserved pre-1860 Bohemian enameled glassware can be mistaken for Moser decorated items dating from a later period. Unknown maker. Height 11⁵⁄₈", c. 1830–40.

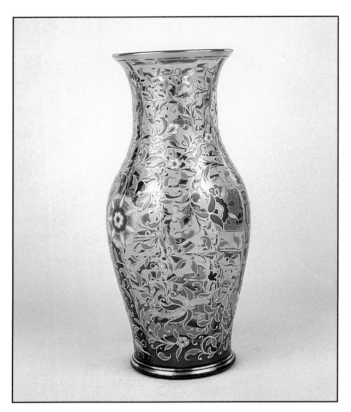

Plate 243 Enameling on this Theresienthal Römer could be mistaken for a product of the Heckert or Moser factories. Height 6¼", c. 1900.

Plate 244 Stylized floral patterns employed by Theresienthal decorators are similar to stylized forms found on Moser glassware. Attributed to Theresienthal. Height 8¼", c. 1900.

Plate 245 Collection of pre-1860 European glassware illustrating various enameled decorative styles by unknown makers. *Left to right:* delicately enameled lavender opaline vase, French or Bohemian, c. 1840–50 est.; Biedermeier uranium glass cologne bottle (Annegelb) with scrollwork and floral enameling, c. 1830–40; blue opaline cologne bottle with early gold over antique white enamel decoration, Bohemia, c. 1840–60.

VIII. Moser? Perhaps, Perhaps Not!

PROBLEMS OF IDENTIFICATION

Uncertainty! Uncertainty is a major factor surrounding our very existence. In trying to unravel the mysteries associated with the proper attribution of Central European artistic glass, uncertainty is particularly relevant. It is the intention of this chapter to highlight the numerous difficulties encountered when trying to identify Moser glassware, to provide illustrative examples indicating the type of cooperative efforts which apparently existed between Moser and other independent glasshouses and decorators and to provide a sampling of the most commonly found glassware produced by rival firms which resemble Moser artistic glass styles.

Most glassware produced in the second half of the 19th century was unmarked as to the company of origin. Glassware was generally sold with paper labels which either specified the company that manufactured the item or the company or retail outlet that sold it. For purposes of attribution, finding an original paper label today is indeed a rare occurrence. As one progresses into the 20th century, more and more glassware was indelibly signed.

Unfortunately, after World War II and with increasing frequency thereafter, forged signatures were (and are) being applied to popular forms of earlier artistic glass. Loss of factory records, the presence of forged signatures and the frequency with which glasshouses and decorators emulated popular glassware manufactured by rival firms severely complicates the problem of proper identification.

Positive attribution of 19th and early 20th century glassware to Moser decorators is principally confounded by the presence of a forged diamond scribed Moser script signature. This signature is the one most commonly found on Moser style glass and was definitely employed by the Moser factory; however, its mode of application and stylistic simplicity have made it a major forgery target for unscrupulous profit seekers. Uncertainty as to the validity of the script signature, when trying to establish the attribution of undocumented artistic glass samples, forms the underlying motivation for the inclusion of this chapter.

In spite of the complexity and competitive nature of the Bohemian art glass industry, articles produced by the Moser firm are of a sufficiently distinctive character that proper attribution is possible for a reasonable percentage of the examples encountered. A few of the more notable exceptions include German neo-Renaissance glass, ungilded enameled glass, aquatic style glassware and engraved glass which, without the benefit of a reliable signature, can be extremely difficult to associate with a specific manufacturer.

Source identification and date of manufacturer are both required to establish the full provenance of a particular article. Clues to the dating of artistic glass can originate from a multiplicity of sources. Factory records and catalogs provide irrefutable proof of provenance but are in many instances either missing completely or at best reveal only fragmentary information. Factory marks and artist signatures, while providing valuable evidence, require specialized knowledge which can only be confirmed through historic records. Stylistic epochs, such as the Second Rococo and Biedermeier, and their associated glass types and forms, cutting and engraving styles and decorative motifs represent the front line of attack in dating examples for which no documented evidence exists.

Glass types and forms employed by Moser prior to the opening of the Meierhöfen works are of little use in identification or dating since they were acquired from various factories located throughout Bohemia. Further, the characteristic Bohemian intransigence in the face of changing world styles was exemplified by early Moser production. Adherence to traditional Biedermeier and Second Rococo/Bohemian Baroque decorative themes, even after the remainder of the Bohemian artistic glass industry had shifted to more progressive forms, was characteristic of Moser glass. Indeed, many of these themes remained popular well into the 20th century and were utilized in various forms up until World War II. Even though Moser glass produced during the latter half of the 19th century was distinctive, accurate dating is complicated by the longevity of many of the decorative themes employed. Fortunately, a rather complete set of Moser factory records for the 1910–1933 period were brought to the United States by Leo Moser.[1] Although, only covering artistic glass created at Meierhöfen and

---

[1] Moser factory records reside at the Corning Museum of Glass in Corning, New York.

Meyr's Neffe, these papers provide us with extensive documentation regarding glass types, forms and cutting styles produced during this period. Additional insight into the production of Art Nouveau forms at Meierhöfen can be obtained from various published works. With the interesting exception of enameled glassware, artistic glass production at Meierhöfen and Meyr's Neffe appears to be reasonably well defined.

Enameled glassware produced by the Moser firm remains an enigma. Of the Moser glass available to American collectors, enameled ware represents a significant portion; yet, there is almost a complete lack of recognition of Moser enameled glass in German and Czechoslovakian books and periodicals. There is essentially no reference to enameled glass in the Moser factory records during the tenure of Leo Moser as artistic director. Even though enameled glass was still being produced by Moser after 1930, eyewitness accounts indicate that this type of glass was absent from the major Moser showrooms in the Karlsbad area as well as from the main factory showroom at Meierhöfen. From available evidence, it has been concluded that beginning with the opening of the Meistersdorf decorating facility in 1870, the vast majority of enameled glass produced by the Moser firm was exported to countries outside of the Central European area.

To the collector of fine glass, the foremost criteria to be used in evaluating the intrinsic worth of a particular object should always be artistic design and quality of execution. Fortunately, these characteristics can be easily assessed by a trained or discriminating observer. Factory of origin and date of manufacture, while generally exerting a significant influence over the market value of a particular item, are typically difficult to evaluate and require a considerable depth of knowledge to be accurately determined. Rarity, perhaps the most elusive property of all, must ultimately be based on the number of items available to the collector. Incomplete factory records regarding production quantities, as well as natural attrition over the years, compel one to rely on the frequency with which a particular item appears on the open market to assess this property. Needless to say, such an approach is fraught with difficulties and inaccuracy, and one can indeed be treading a fine line by declaring a particular form to be rare. Articles of glass which can be attributed to a specific manufacturer are of extreme importance to a glass historian and, in the case of signed examples, can influence market value. One must be careful, however, not to lose sight of the artistic significance of a piece in deference to its possessing an identifiable signature. Quality, more than any other factor, should remain of paramount importance in determining ultimate value.

MOSER—MULTINATIONAL COOPERATIVE EFFORTS

As a major European glass decorating house, Moser was in a unique position to develop extensive commercial relationships with other glasshouses both locally and internationally. Although documented details relating to such business ventures are not presently available, sufficiently strong evidence exists, in some cases, that positive conclusions are possible. In this context, the following paragraphs explore the probable business relationships which existed between Moser and Meyr's Neffe, J. & L. Lobmeyr, Salviati & Co., The Venice & Murano Glass Co., Cristalleries de St.-Louis and Mühlhaus (Nový Bor). Less likely, but equally interesting, is a possible association between Moser and the Fostoria Co. (USA).

MOSER, MEYR'S NEFFE, AND J. & L. LOBMEYR

Prior to World War I, Meyr's Neffe was a significant contributor to the field of Bohemian artistic glass; yet, Meyr's Neffe remains a virtual unknown among American collectors. This lack of recognition can largely be attributed to the fact that a major portion of the artistic glass produced at Meyr's Neffe's Adolf works was actually marketed in the United States by the Viennese based firm of J. & L. Lobmeyr. By the 1880s, J. & L. Lobmeyr had developed into the foremost glass merchandising organization in Europe. Sadly, due to inadequate manufacturing facilities and a shortage of glass decorators in the Vienna area, it became dependent for its survival on an extensive network of design and production facilities situated throughout Austria and Bohemia. In addition to a permanent staff of designers, Lobmeyr commissioned original works from Central European artists and design groups which were subsequently executed by Bohemian factories. The necessity of a close liaison with Bohemian factories is attested to by the fact that when Austria and Bohemia were separated in 1918, Stefan Rath, the acting director of J. & L. Lobmeyr prior to World War I, left Vienna to found a glassworks, the J. & L. Lobmeyr's Neffe Stefan Rath, in Steinschönau.

When Ludwig Lobmeyr engaged Meyr's Neffe to produce neo-Renaissance type glassware in the late 1860s, Ludwig Moser represented a comparatively unrecognized portion of the Bohemian artistic glass industry. With the opening of the Meistersdorf refinery, this situation was dramatically altered. By the middle 1870s Moser glass had gained international prominence and, with Ludwig Moser's subsequent appointment as supplier to the Austrian Imperial Court, rose to a preeminent position with respect to rival Bohemian glasshouses. With these developments, the marketing acumen of Ludwig Lobmeyr would have required the consideration of Moser as a potential supplier of artistic glass to the Lobmeyr firm. An additional and possibly consequential factor was the timely marriage of Ludwig Moser to Julie Meyer. Even in the face of these intriguing circumstances, evidence suggests that Moser and Lobmeyr remained competitors until Moser purchased Meyr's Neffe's Adolf works in 1922. After that, Lobmeyr apparently continued to market glass produced at the Adolf works. Occasionally, one finds glassware dating from this later period which is co-signed "Moser and Lobmeyr." Plate 156 illustrates a co-signed, engraved goblet originally designed by Stefan Rath and belonging to Lobmeyr's table set No. 253. A distinctive Moser 19th–20th century decorative style is quite evident on the tumbler in Plate 153; however, this example bears a gold Lobmeyr signature and was probably produced at the Adolf works after 1922.

Enameled glassware produced by Moser and Meyr's Neffe bear a strong resemblance to each other. Indeed, as mentioned in the following paragraphs, identical decorative motifs were employed by both firms. Glass blanks decorated by Moser, prior to the opening of the Meierhöfen facility, were predominantly purchased from Meyr's Neffe. When Moser opened the Meierhöfen glassworks, Meyr's Neffe was instrumental in providing the managerial and technical expertise necessary for its guaranteed success. In 1922, the firms of Moser and Meyr's Neffe merged their resources. All things considered, one must agree with the observation of Dr. Alena Adlerová that, prior to 1922, Moser and Meyr's Neffe operated in a cooperative atmosphere. Unfortunately, the precise business relationships which existed between the two firms cannot presently be defined.

MOSER, THE VENICE & MURANO GLASS CO. AND SALVIATI & CO.

Unraveling the commercial relationships which existed between various European glass manufacturers is like reading an Agatha Christie mystery novel. Clues appear one by one until, at last, the mystery appears to be solved. Such was the experience encountered while studying the potential association between Moser and two of the most prominent Venetian (Muranese) glassmaking houses; The Venice & Murano Glass Co. and Salviati & Co. Much previously unidentified glassware, produced around the turn-of-the-century, can be traced to the cooperative efforts of these companies.

Historically, The Venice & Murano Glass Co. and Salviati & Co. were closely related. When a revival of the once famous Venetian glass industry occurred during the second half of the 19th century, the Vicenzan lawyer Antonio Salviati opened his first glass workshop in 1866. This enterprise, which became known as the Venice and Murano Glass and Mosaic Co. Ltd., included glassmasters from the Barovier, Seguso and Moretti families. Early financial difficulties forced Salviati into partnership with an English-based holding company. This association was dissolved in 1878 when Salviati withdrew to found a new glassworks. Salviati's original firm, renamed The Venice & Murano Glass Co., retained the services of the Barovier family while the Segusos and Morettis joined Salviati's new company. In 1896, the Camerino family acquired control of the Salviati glassworks, then known by the name Salviati & Co.-Venice.

Adherence to family traditions has always been of great importance to Muranese glass blowers and artists. It was from these roots that classical soda-lime (Venetian glass) glass forms, for which the Muranese masters gained international fame during the 18th century, were reintroduced after 1860. From a financial standpoint, this rebirth proved quite successful. Technically, the parallel development of improved refining techniques and new glass colors provided a firm foundation for the innovative 20th century Muranese glass industry which was to follow. A less desirable side effect of Muranese tradition was the inability to rapidly adapt to changing glass styles.

After 1890, Art Nouveau and other progressive art forms registered dramatic gains in international popularity. During this period the Muranese glass industry largely continued to produce 18th century designs. It was not until 1910 that a significant break with traditional artistic styles could be recognized.

Prior to 1895, Moser functioned solely as a glass decorating workshop. After 1870, major emphasis was placed on the production of enameled glassware for specialized world markets. When Moser's glass manufactory at Meierhöfen opened in 1895, the Moser decorating workshop was primarily occupied with the cutting and engraving of newly developed, high quality glass blanks. In order to support the remaining body of artists and enamelists, Moser continued to enamel glass blanks acquired from major glasshouses throughout Europe.

Meanwhile, the Muranese glass industry was feeling the effects of reduced demand for the more traditional Venetian forms. To bolster sales, popular contemporary glassware produced by other manufacturers was incorporated into their product lines. For example, Pauly & Cie., a Venetian glasshouse, imported glassware by Tiffany, Gallé, Daum, Löetz and Moser for sale throughout Italy. Glass manufactured by Moser, Graff Harrach and other Bohemian/Silesian firms is pictured, along with traditional Venetian forms, in a Salviati & Co. catalog published around the turn-of-the-century. Moser's necessity of maintaining a decorative workshop at full capacity, in combination with the greater commercial popularity of Central European decorative designs, logically set the stage for a cooperative effort between Venetian glass manufacturers and Moser decorators.

Salviati & Co. and The Venice & Murano Glass Co. were two firms which ostensibly employed the services of Moser decorators. Plate 115 illustrates an enameled foliate and canine decorative pattern which originated in 16th century Spain. In one instance, this decoration is applied to an identifiable Salviati blank while, in the other, the blank is typically Central European. Both Venetian and Central European blanks with this decorative motif have been found with Moser signatures.

Bohemia/Silesian cranberry or shaded glass blanks consist of colored glass sandwiched between two layers of clear Bohemian crystal. Two such examples appear in Plate 118. Of particular interest is the gilded decorative pattern applied to the cup and saucer, and decanter. This particular pattern can also be found in a Salviati catalog of the period. Decoration of this type (known as "Graffito" in Italian), was created by scratching away a layer of pure gold foil with a sharp instrument. Salviati was known for employing artists who were well-versed in the use of Graffito; however, records indicate that the patterns created by Salviati emphasized ancient or paleo-Christian themes. In contrast, the Graffito patterns illustrated in this book are primarily based on Judaic themes or Baroque patterns found on 18th century Bohemian Zwischengoldglas (gold patterns encased between two layers of crystal; see Plate 26 in *Czechoslovakian Glass*).

Ruby glass was popular among Muranese glasshouses during the last quarter of the 19th century. Plate 205 illustrates a signed Venice & Murano Glass

Co. finger bowl and underplate, made from a highly refined ruby glass blank, decorated with a Baroque foliate-scroll Graffito pattern. Additional examples of decorated Venetian ruby glass are shown in Plate 114. All of these examples exhibit a rather distinctive glass coloration under ultraviolet (UV) light. When exposed to short-wavelength UV radiation from a mercury source (254 nanometers), the inside surfaces exhibit a uniform, pale yellow-orange, powdery fluorescence while the outside surfaces show bright to pale yellow-orange, marble-like striations. This characteristic is most likely related to a specific manufacturing procedure. Since not all Venetian ruby glass exhibits this unusual property, it is highly probable that The Venice & Murano Glass Co. manufactured all glass blanks which fall into this category. If this premise is correct, The Venice & Murano Glass Co. manufactured an extensive variety of decorated artistic glass which falls under the general category of "Venetian Style" glassware (refer to Chapters Six and Seven for further information on decorative characteristics of Venetian Style glassware). Careful study of over 20 examples of this glassware strongly indicates a common source for the applied decoration. Artistic properties of the enamel work and gilded Graffito were extremely consistent among all examples investigated. Plate 113 illustrates a deep ruby vase, facet-cut and of form #M/7734 as identified in the Moser sketch book; decoration is unmistakably in the Venetian Style. This example alone leaves little doubt that Moser decorators were responsible for Venetian Style glassware.

Moser signatures occur only rarely on Venetian Style glassware. When they do occur they are diamond scribed and appear to be isolated to those examples which do not feature distinctly Venetian themes (i.e., canal scenes). Examples of this type may have been retained by Moser for Central European consumption or for export to other countries. It is most likely that glassware decorated with Venetian scenes was returned by Moser to The Venice & Murano Glass Co. for sale throughout Italy.

All things taken into consideration—the reliance of Venetian glassmaking houses on Central European glass design to bolster their receding share of the luxury glass market, the need for the Moser firm to financially support its large body of glass decorators, the well-established commercial ties between the Bohemian and Venetian glass industries, the occurrence of identical Bohemian design elements on both Bohemian and Venetian glass blanks, and the presence of Moser signatures on various representative examples strongly supports the conclusion that Venetian Style glassware was decorated at Moser workshops. Salviati glassware decorated by Moser dates to the turn of the century. Moser decorated glassware from The Venice & Murano Glass Co. most probably dates from the same period.

MOSER AND CRISTALLERIES de ST.-LOUIS

As recorded in *Moser—Artistry in Glass, 1857–1938*, Plates 150, 182 and 194 illustrate several distinctively decorated items of tableware. Common to each of these examples is the use of a gilded acid cutback decorative pattern on a lead crystal blank. It is not uncommon to find tableware of this type bearing a diamond-scribed script Moser signature. This latter factor, in combination with Leo Moser's declaration that no lead crystal was produced in Bohemia prior to 1916, is what led to a Moser attribution and an estimated date of manufacture of circa 1920–1930. Recently, additional research has significantly altered this conclusion. Tableware of the type referenced above, as well as additional examples discussed in the following paragraphs, was actually produced in Lorraine, Germany around the turn of the century.

Over many years, the geographical area known as Alsace-Lorraine had been a source of contention between Germany and France. At the conclusion of the Franco-Prussian War in 1871, a portion of Lorraine was remanded to Germany; after 1918, this parcel of land was returned to France. During the 1871–1918 period, Lorraine, Germany encompassed three major glassmaking concerns: Cristalleries de St.-Louis (at Münzthal, or, in French, 'D'Argental), Burgun, Schverer and Cie (at Meisenthal) and Vallérysthal. Although each of these firms was noted for its production of art glass, their combined international reputation rested firmly on a vast array of luxury tableware products which, among others, was produced for restaurants, hotels, railroads and steamship lines.

Cristalleries de St.-Louis was established in the town of Münzthal as early as 1586. Destroyed during the Thirty Years War, St.-Louis was reopened in 1767 under the patronage of Louis XV. As early as 1831, St.-Louis opened a retail shop in Paris which, for 25 years, featured a wide range of blown and cut tableware. With the annexation of Lorraine by Germany in 1871, St.-Louis found itself isolated from prior commercial outlets and from much of the French glass industry. However, in spite of these inconveniences, St.-Louis continued its well established tradition of high quality glass produc-

tion. Figure 75 illustrates two examples of tableware produced at Cristalleries de St.-Louis around 1900. These items are characterized by the use of precise cutting techniques, high quality lead crystal blanks, star-cut bases designed to hide pontil marks, and a gilded Rococo-floral acid cut-back decorative pattern.

While the gilded decorative pattern in Fig. 75 is distinctive and potentially would be quite useful in identifying Cristalleries de St.-Louis glassware, it is *not* found exclusively on St.-Louis products. The origin of this Rococo-floral decorative pattern is unknown to the author; however, in addition to St.-Louis, it has been found on Bohemian glassware of undefined origin, glassware produced by the Dorflinger Co. in the United States and by Burgun, Schverer and Cie (Lorraine).

Figure D-71 in *Dorflinger—America's Finest Glass, 1852–1921* by John Quentin Feller illustrates a decanter decorated with a Rococo-floral pattern. This example, which is on display at the Corning Museum of Glass, is similar in form and essentially identical in decoration to the decanter in Fig. 75. According to Feller, the pattern on the Corning decanter was applied by Carl Prosch (or an assistant) at the Honesdale Decorating Co. (c. 1903) and was given the name "Puerto Rico." Prior to his immigration to the United States, Christian Dorflinger served an eight year apprenticeship at Cristalleries de St.-Louis. Since St.-Louis finishing and decorative influences are evident on much of the glass produced by Dorflinger, this link probably explains the strong similarity between the Dorflinger and St.-Louis decanters.

Burgun, Schverer and Cie was considered to be one of the finest glasshouses in Europe. On page 16 of *The Glass of Désiré Christian* by Jules S. Traub is a reprint of a page out of Anton Burgun's personal copy of Burgun, Schverer and Cie's 1900 catalog. In this reprint is a sketch of a footed shallow bowl bearing the same Rococo-floral decorative motif pictured in Fig. 75.

For the Rococo-floral pattern illustrated in Fig. 75, it is quite evident that the attribution of glassware to a specific manufacturer, solely based on this decorative pattern and style of execution, can lead to difficulties.

The lead crystal wine goblet to the left in Plate 206 has an air-twist facet-cut stem and a cased distinctively colored citrone bowl; in the middle is a similar wine goblet with a cased green bowl. Neither wine goblet has a star-cut foot since manufacturing techniques employed would not have placed a pontil mark at that point. Based on decorative patterns alone, these two examples warrant a Cristalleries de St.-Louis attribution. To the right in Plate 206 is a lead crystal wine goblet with a cased cit-

Fig. 75 Lead crystal tableware with a gilded acid cut-back Baroque floral pattern. Attributed to St.-Louis, c. 1900. Lid of pitcher is 800 silver and marked with the German Crown & Crescent, height 12".

rone bowl identical in coloration to the goblet on the left. This goblet retains its original paper label "Made in Lorraine, Germany." Plate 207 illustrates a cased lead crystal sherbet and underplate and dessert plate in the same citrone colored glass noted in Plate 206; each of these examples has a star-cut base. While the cordial goblet in Plate 207 bears the same gilded acid cut-back pattern as the other examples in the figure, the green coloration of the bowl is identical to the goblet in the middle of Plate 206. Under a black light (short wavelength, 254 nanometers; long wavelength, 366 nanometers), the short or long wavelength fluorescence of the citrone or green colored examples in Plates 206 and 207 are identical. As an aggregate, evidence strongly indicates that the tableware pictured in these plates shares a common point of manufacture.

It was an accepted practice for glasshouses, when they received orders exceeding their production capacity, to subcontract rival firms to produce the required glassware. For those companies concentrated in Lorraine, Germany, one would logically expect that such subcontracts would primarily remain local. It must be remembered, however, that around the turn of the century the firm of Ludwig Moser & Sons had an excess decorating capacity, specialized in the decoration of glass blanks provided by other glasshouses, and was internationally known for the quality of their decorative styles.

Further evidence of Moser involvement with the Lorraine glass industry is provided by the example in Plate 67. Each element of this lead crystal water set bears what appears to be a genuine Moser acid-etched signature. An identical water set, having a slightly different acid cut-back decorative pattern, and dated 1875, is attributed to Cristalleries de St.-Louis in *British Glass, 1800–1914* by Charles R. Hajdamach (Plate 187, on page 197).

Presented evidence strongly favors Cristalleries de

St.-Louis as producer of the tableware discussed in these paragraphs. One cannot overlook the fact, however, that each of the three glasshouses located in Lorraine, Germany were capable of producing similar quality glassware, were located in close proximity to each other and probably shared production of popular glassware styles. For these reasons, a positive St.-Louis attribution for all examples presented must remain somewhat in question.

There is a high probability that Ludwig Moser & Sons was involved in the decoration of glass produced by at least one firm located in Lorraine, Germany. Some of this decorated glassware appears to have been retained by the Moser firm and sold under their own name. A commercial venture of this type would explain the presence of Moser signatures on lead crystal glassware produced prior to 1916.

MOSER AND MÜHLHAUS (NOVÝ BOR)

Founded by Julius Mühlhaus in 1867, the Mühlhaus glass refinery in Nový Bor was recognized as one of the most prominent decorating workshops in northern Bohemia. According to contemporary Czech sources, Mühlhaus produced a line of artistic glassware which featured dense patterns of naturalistic themes executed in gold and platinum as well as Mary Gregory style enameling. Representative examples, such as those illustrated on page 92 of *Collectible Bohemian Glass*, by Robert and Deborah Truitt are virtually indistinguishable from similar glassware marketed by Moser.

In reviewing contemporary and period reference sources, several rather interesting factors come to light. The Moser refinery at Meistersdorf and the Mühlhaus refinery at Nový Bor were geographically located in close proximity to each other. Both Moser and Mühlhaus purchased high quality glass blanks from Harrach, Meyr's Neffe and Löetz. Czech records show that Mühlhaus was granted permission to use the Austrian Imperial Eagle on his seal in 1872; Moser became supplier of glass to the Imperial Court in the same time period and, as illustrated in Fig. 95, used the Austrian Imperial Eagle on their paper label during the latter half of the 19th century. Plate 65 illustrates a Mary Gregory style enameled vase which could easily have been produced by Mühlhaus but which has its original Moser Austrian Imperial Eagle paper label intact.

Dr. Alena Adlerová, in her booklet on Moser glass, suggests that a second refinery, in addition to Moser's Meistersdorf refinery, was probably responsible for decorating some of the glassware marketed by Moser. When the demand for a specific product line exceeded productive capacity, it was a common practice for glasshouses to subcontract work to rival firms.

Consideration of the above factors leads to the conclusion that Mühlhaus probably produced decorated artistic glass for the Moser firm and, when the opportunity presented itself, may well have marketed it under their own name.

MOSER AND FOSTORIA (USA)?

One of the major problems facing the United States' artistic glass industry during the last quarter of the 19th and first quarter of the 20th centuries, was the opinion held by many American consumers that artistic glass imported from Europe was of better value than glass produced at home. Apparently, there was some truth in this assumption since some United States glasshouses found it less expensive to import quality glass blanks from Europe than to produce them locally.

Plate 205 illustrates an acid cut-back and gilded cranberry dessert bowl and underplate. The glass blank employed in this example is composed of three cased layers of glass, exhibits the dominant Bohemian crystal fluorescence coloration described in Chapter 7, has a twisted-panel structure characteristic of Central European glass and was most probably produced in Czechoslovakia. Of particular interest is the acid-etched scene surrounding the bowl and underplate. This etched pattern is one of three variations from the "Wild Life" series designed by Edgar Mott Bottome for the Wheeling Decorating Co. Wheeling, West Virginia, in the 1920s (ref. the *Morgantown Newscaster*, Vol. 4, No. 1). These decorative patterns were applied to Fostoria, Morgantown and imported Bohemian (Czechoslovakian) glass blanks.

Tableware (i.e., bowls, plates and goblets) decorated in the style illustrated in Plate 205 are occasionally found bearing a script Moser signature. Signed examples are generally constructed from ruby or green colored glass. When evaluating a signed Moser cased cranberry soda goblet, a noted authority on acid-etched Fostoria glass commented that the acid cutting was done using a two-step process which added to the quality of the piece. This observation indicates that, at least for the sample examined, the signed Moser goblet exhibited a higher quality of workmanship than was normally encountered with glassware produced by Fostoria. Once again the frequency with which forged script Moser signatures are encountered muddies the attribution waters. Limited evidence indicates that Moser may have contracted Fostoria to produce glassware to their specification or obtained the rights to produce glassware using Wheeling Decorating Co. designs. Although unlikely, the possibility remains that this type of glassware was produced in its entirety by the Fostoria Co.

SIMILAR PRODUCTS
PRODUCED BY RIVAL FIRMS

Bohemia is composed of a geographically isolated land area approximately the size of Pennsylvania. Within its confines, the 19th and early 20th centuries witnessed what was perhaps the greatest concentration of manufacturers engaged in the production of artistic glass to be found anywhere in the world. Since much of the artistic glass produced in Central Europe was never signed, it is no wonder that associating artistic styles with specific firms can be problematic. Evaluating the extent to which rival Bohemian glasshouses adopted each other's profitable product lines presents a formidable task. Problems of this nature can be appreciated by considering a microcosm of the glass industry which existed in the Haida-Steinschönau region of northern Bohemia.[2]

Although decorating workshops were associated with many major glass manufacturing houses, a considerable portion of their raw glass output was distributed by independent glass dealers to local groups of "home workers." These groups would, in turn, be responsible for decorating the glass and returning it to the dealers for marketing. Home worker organizations rarely exceeded 15 members, yet, in 1900, it is recorded that over 60 percent of the total number of glass decorators employed in the Haida-Steinschönau area fell under this classification. Complementing this extensive home industry were major glass decorating firms which, within the 1900–1930 time frame, included such names as Beyermann & Co. (Haida), Conrath & Liebsch (Steinschönau), Carl Goldberg (Haida), Hartmann & Dieterichs (Haida), Carl Hosch (Haida), W. Kulka (Haida), Gebr. Lorenz (Steinschönau), Carl Meltzer & Co. (Langenau), Julius Mühlhaus & Co. (Haida), Joh. Oertel & Co. (Haida), Gebr. Pallme-König (Steinschönau), Friedrich Pietsch (Steinschönau), Brüder Rachmann (Haida), Carl Schappel (Haida) and Tschernich & Co. (Haida).

The following paragraphs list several European manufacturers of artistic glass which produced items closely resembling those marketed by Moser. This listing is by no means complete, but serves the purpose of acquainting Moser collectors with the diversity of similar high quality glassware produced by rival firms.

Thomas Webb & Sons, Stourbridge, England

Plate 130 in *Moser—Artistry in Glass* illustrates a rainbow glass bowl with Moser-type enameled scrollwork surrounding the rim. Because of this enameled decor, the example cited was previously attributed to Moser. However, this vase, which is illustrated in Plate 211, was actually produced by Thomas Webb & Sons. A cased version of Webb rainbow glass is also shown in Plate 211.

Plate 162 illustrates three Moser wine goblets with rainbow glass bowls. Moser rainbow glass is visually indistinguishable from rainbow glass produced by other manufacturers. To date, glass fluorescence, has been the only positive approach to identifying unsigned examples. In the case of Webb rainbow glass, all examples tested exhibit a strong green fluorescence typical of uranium in the melt. This characteristic is not present in Moser rainbow glass.

Webb produced enameled glassware which, in some cases, is virtually indistinguishable in style, decorative motif and technique of execution, from similar items produced by Moser. Webb employed the composite enamel-gilt decorating technique, widely employed by Moser decorators, as described in Chapter Six ("Enameled Glass"), emphasized naturalistic themes such as flowers, insects and aquatic life forms and employed Bohemian style Baroque scrollwork in their decorative designs. Typically, Webb designs are worked on opaque single layer or cased glass blanks; Moser designs are more often found on single layer or cased transparent blanks. Plate 209 presents a cased and shaded Webb enameled vase which illustrates a floral and insect decorative motif of exceptional quality. Plate 210 shows a Webb vase with a floral-centered diaper-work motif executed in the composite enamel-gilt technique.

Meyr's Neffe, Winterberg (Vimperk), Bohemia

Meyr's Neffe employed many of the finest enamelists, glass cutters and engravers to be found in Central Europe. In addition, Meyr's Neffe was the primary supplier of enameled and engraved glass to the world renowned glass marketing firm of J. & L. Lobmeyr. Glassware marketed by J. & L. Lobmeyer, and consequently Meyr's Neffe, is considered by many to repre-

---

[2]Moser's Meistersdorf decorating facility was located within this geographical area.

sent some of the finest quality artistic glass ever produced.

Differentiating between artistic glass produced by Moser and Meyr's Neffe, prior to their merger in 1922, can be quite difficult. Plate 203 illustrates a heavily decorated beaker with a distinctive cartouche, outlined with white enamel dots, accenting enameled foliate patterns. Comparison of this decorative style with the decanter in Plate 201 (this decanter was also illustrated in Plate 29 of *Moser—Artistry in Glass*), indicates a common point of manufacture. Claude V. Cox, on page 29 of his booklet entitled *Ludwig Moser, Royal Glass Artisan, 1833–1916*, attributes a similarly decorated decanter to the Moser firm. Although there is little doubt that the decorative style illustrated in Plates 201 and 203 was produced by Moser and/or Meyr's Neffe, there is still insufficient documentation to make a positive attribution of the decanter.

Glassware decorated in the Acanthus Ornamentation style is known to have been marketed concurrently by J. & L. Lobmeyr, Meyr's Neffe, Moser, Harrach and, perhaps, several additional Bohemian firms. Based on current knowledge, the glassware decorated in the style illustrated in Plate 204, which has been attributed to Moser by American collectors, was either produced at Meyr's Neffe's Adolf works or by Graff Harrach.

J. & L. Lobmeyr marketed a particular style of beautifully enameled and gilded glassware which was manufactured by Meyr's Neffe; Plate 199 illustrates a wine goblet executed in this readily recognizable decorative motif. Plate 199 also shows a similarly decorated cup and saucer which is signed in gold block letters "MOSER." Close scrutiny of these two examples shows a slight variation in the quality of execution; however, without the benefit of a Moser signature, the cup and saucer would have unquestionably been attributed to Lobmeyr (Meyr's Neffe).

Meyr's Neffe produced historical glass forms decorated in Schwarzlot. Although this type of glass decoration is quite distinctive, its intricate detailing could easily lead to an erroneous Moser attribution. Plate 202 illustrates a Meyr's Neffe pokal decorated in the chinoiserie (Chinese-like) schwarzlot style made famous by Ignaz Preissler.[3]

Graff Harrach, Neuwelt (Nový Svět), Bohemia

Graff Harrach is one of the oldest Bohemian glasshouses still in operation and, since its founding, has been world renowned for the high quality artistic glassware produced there. Harrach is also noted for producing a tremendously diverse range of glassware and was not above emulating products produced by rival glasshouses both at home and abroad.

Harrach was a major producer of engraved Art Nouveau glass quite similar to that produced by Moser. Plate 215 compares engraved Art Nouveau vases produced by Moser and Harrach. These vases are of similar heavyweight construction; however, close comparison reveals several distinctive differences. In contrast to the gradual shading of clear to color (bottom to top) exhibited by the Moser vases, the Harrach example shades from a deeper coloration to clear with a rather abrupt change in shading. Engraving on the Moser vase is noticeably deeper than on its Harrach counterpart, and, in general, Moser engraved forms are proportionally larger in scale than those employed by Harrach.

Plate 132 compares a Harrach engraved Art Nouveau vase with gilded highlights to a Moser Art Nouveau vase; both vases were executed on a Bohemian Crystal blank. Harrach engraved Art Nouveau glassware often exhibits gilded highlights within the engraved motif. Examples of Moser engraved Art Nouveau glass with similar gilded highlights are unknown to the author. In addition, the distinctive gold-enamel decoration employed at the base and rim of the Harrach examples in Plates 212, 213 and 215 appears to be a unique characteristic of Harrach production. One final note in identifying Harrach engraved Art Nouveau glass; Harrach glassware generally has a shallow engraved letter, followed by two or more numbers, on the base.

Tiffany (USA), Webb and Stevens & Williams (England), Moser and Graff Harrach were major producers of high quality Art Nouveau glassware embellished with marquetry insets. Plates 123 and 124 illustrate several examples of Moser marquetry glass. Typically, Moser marquetry insets are constructed from one or two cased layers of cameo-cut glass. This type of construction provides a shaded inset with a subtle range of colors. With the possible exception of Karlsbader Secession glass (Plate 135), Moser rarely combined multiple colored marquetry insets in a single piece of glassware. Graff Harrach, on the other hand, produced marquetry in a multiplicity of color combinations (Plate 213).

Harrach produced aquatic theme glassware which,

---

[3] A similar pokal to that pictured in Plate 202 resides at the Corning Museum of Glass in Corning, New York.

without the benefit of an authentic signature is virtually impossible to differentiate from similar glassware thought to have been produced by Moser. Plates 218 and 221 illustrate two examples of aquatic theme glassware produced by Harrach.

Moser is noted for its production of facet-cut Art Deco glassware featuring gilded cameo-cut friezes executed in various patterns. The most common cameo pattern encountered is the Amazon Warrior frieze illustrated in Fig. 60. Harrach, as well as several other Bohemian glasshouses, also produced Art Deco glassware using cameo friezes. In general, frieze decorated Moser glassware is signed in script on the base. In the absence of a signature, either the cameo pattern or the specific shape of the item must be known to warrant a Moser attribution.

Harrach employed some of the finest enamelists working in Bohemia. While some of Harrach's enameled patterns are highly intricate and reminiscent of Moser enameling styles (Plates 216 and 217), the themes employed were sufficiently removed from the mainstream of Moser production that misattributions occur only infrequently.

Plate 96 illustrates a signed Moser decanter set decorated in the French Empire style. This type of decoration is atypical of Moser enameled glassware found in the United States and was probably intended for the French market. Plate 214 displays a cologne bottle with a red marquetry inset (like the insets employed by Moser for their Karlsbader Secession glassware) and French Empire style enameling similar to the decanter set in Plate 96; the cologne bottle was manufactured by Graff Harrach.

Fritz Heckert (Silesia)

Founded in 1866, the Fritz Heckert glasshouse in Warmbrunn, Silesia, produced enameled glassware of outstanding quality. Principally known for their historically accurate rendition of German neo-Renaissance glass during the 1880s, and the distinctive naturalistic enameled designs executed by Max Rade, Fritz Heckert produced intricately enameled, gilded and jeweled Bohemian crystal glassware which could easily be confused with products of the Moser firm. Plate 224 illustrates a signed Fritz Heckert wine goblet displaying an intricate pattern executed in two-color gold. Moser is well known for the use of enameled birds and insects. As illustrated in Plate 223, Fritz Heckert also employed these decorative accents. Plate 225 shows a stained amber Bohemian crystal chalice decorated with composite gold-enamel and applied glass jewels. Stained amber Bohemian crystal occurs quite often as a decorative element on Fritz Heckert glassware. Also illustrated is an enameled Rococo style wine goblet (Plate 224) and a cut and enameled vase (Plate 225). The decorative motif and the use of composite gold enameling techniques on these examples bears a close resemblance to similar ware produced by Moser.

Josephinenhütte (Silesia)

Josephinenhütte, located in Schrieberhau, Riesengebirge, was establish in 1842 by Count Leopold Schaffgotsch and operated under the artistic directorship of Franz Pohl (1813–1884). Josephinenhütte specialized in fine quality Bohemian crystal tableware and decorative vases. Glassware produced by the firms of Fritz Heckert and Josephinenhütte represent the vast majority of Silesian artistic glass available to the American collector. Both glasshouses produced glassware equal in quality to the best produced by Bohemian manufacturers. In 1923, Josephinenhütte merged with the firms of Fritz Heckert and Neumann & Staebe (Hermsdorf, Kynast) to form the Petersdorf based joint stock company which traded by the name JO-HE-KY.

Plate 226 illustrates a Josephinenhütte ewer richly decorated in platinum and gold. Islamic style decoration was employed by Moser and other Bohemian glasshouses in the 1880s. A three-handled Islamic style loving cup produced by Josephinenhütte, is shown in Plate 227. Josephinenhütte employed Baroque and floral decorative patterns similar to those employed by Moser decorators; Plate 228 presents two representative examples. Note that the saucer in Plate 228 has a star-cut pattern cut into its base which is not generally present on Moser examples.

Riedel (Polubný-Bohemia)

Tracing its history as far back as the 17th century, the Riedel family represents a long standing tradition of quality glassmakers. Perhaps best known for uranium colored glasses developed by Josef Riedel, Sr. (1816–1894), Riedel glass products can be included with the finest artistic glassware ever produced in Central Europe.

Riedel artisans were experts in the field of facet-cut glass and may have supplied many of the cut glass forms to which friezes of cameo decoration were applied by Moser decorators. Plate 98 in *Riedel Since 1756* illustrates a facet-cut vase identical in form to signed cameo and engraved (Fig. 57) Moser vases.

Riedel employed the enamel decorating services of the Vinzenz Pohl workshops in Neuwelt-Harrachsdorf during the latter quarter of the 19th century; this facility was later absorbed by the Riedel firm. Plate 230 shows a pair of tall green goblets with enamel/coralene decoration which are attributed to the Pohl workshops, circa 1880. Plate 231 illustrates a tankard decorated with a gold peacock and schwarzlot type enameling. This example could easily be attributed to Moser or, even more likely, to Meyr's Neffe; however, it was produced by Riedel around the turn of the century. Plate 230 shows a Riedel enameled vase, produced around 1893, which exhibits high-relief Baroque scrollwork similar to that found on the pair of Moser vases in Plate 47.

Rössler (Bohemia)

Between WWI and WWII, Theodore Rössler produced enameled glassware in the Persian style which he referred to as "color cake." As illustrated in Plate 229, Rössler's enameling technique was characterized by the application of thickly contoured enamels to a background which was first outlined using stenciled patterns in dull gold enamel. Glass blanks employed by Rössler typically exhibit closely spaced optical ribbing. Rössler's "color cake" enameling can be easily confused with similar 19th century glassware produced by Gallé in France or marketed by Lobmeyr in Vienna. The use of a stenciled outline and background pattern is also reminiscent of the large floral enameled glassware produced by Moser. Examples of Rössler's glassware have been found with a script Moser signature; based on present information however, these signatures are most likely forgeries.

Löetz (Klöstermühle, Bohemia)

Löetz is internationally recognized for manufacturing some of the highest quality iridescent Art Nouveau glassware even produced. What few collectors realize, however, is that around 1890 Löetz also produced a line of enameled glassware which, in many instances, could easily be misattributed as products of the Moser firm. Plate 234 illustrates a melon-ribbed "Carneol" footed vase with an enameled Moser style rim decoration. Plate 232 shows a Löetz enameled vase in the "Agate" pattern while Plates 233 and 235 illustrate floral decorative patterns applied to iridescent glass blanks.

Kulka (Nový Bor)

In 1917, Wenzel Kulka opened a glass refinery in Nový Bor, northern Bohemia. Kulka specialized in the production of facet-cut glassware in the (Vienna) Modern style which bears a strong resemblance to similar glassware produced by Moser. Much of this glassware was designed by Alexander Pfohl. Pfohl also designed glass for Moser in the 1930s. Contemporary Czech records indicate that the glass colors employed by Kulka closely parallel those produced by Moser. Kulka's glass was largely produced for export and should be reasonably available to American collectors.

Carl Hosch (Nový Bor)

Carl Hosch opened a glass refinery in Zákupy in 1864; this facility was moved to Nový Bor in 1868. Initial emphasis was on cut crystal, bronze ornaments and lighting fixtures. After 1893, Carl Hosch's two sons concentrated on developing a worldwide network of retail outlets. Although Hosch employed resident decorators, as well as home decorators, much of the glassware sold under the Hosch name was purchased pre-finished from major Bohemian glasshouses. Many of the items illustrated in a Hosch catalog published around 1905 bear a strong resemblance to similar glassware produced by Moser (refer to pages 74 and 77 in *Collectible Bohemian Glass: 1880–1940* by Robert and Deborah Truitt). Of particular interest is a catalog page illustrating a collection of vases which feature high-relief flowers on a gilded ground. Many of the items in this catalog show a multiplicity of Moser decorative characteristics which have not, up to the present time, been associated with any other Bohemian or Silesian glasshouse.

Glasshouses which purchased finished glass products from rival firms and incorporated them into their own product line were not unique in Europe. Major glasshouses such as Hosch, Salviati, Lobmeyr and Pauley & Cie routinely marketed products produced by other manufacturers. This practice, as in the case of Carl Hosch, complicates the proper attribution of specific glassware and, because records of these commercial relationships are difficult to isolate, in many cases represents a problem which will never be fully resolved.

Goldberg (Nový Bor)

Jointly founded by Carl Goldberg and Josef Kreys in 1891, the Goldberg firm was moved to Nový Bor in 1897. Due to participation in major international exhibitions, Goldberg became recognized as one of the finest glass refineries in Central Europe specializing in all types of decorative glassware. In addition to their own product lines, Goldberg decorated glassware for other companies.

Plate 236 illustrates a facet-cut vase decorated by Goldberg. This example, as well as the container in Plate 237, is representative of the popular (Vienna) Modern decorative form which was produced by many Central European glasshouses including Moser. Goldberg also produced a line of facet-cut glassware decorated with acid cut-back cameo friezes. Examples of Goldberg's cameo friezes (refer to page 48 in *Collectible Bohemian Glass* by Robert and Deborah Truitt) can easily be confused with similar glassware produced by Moser.

Sèvres (France)

Verrerie de Sèvres was founded during the reign of Louis XV and was renamed Cristellerie de Sèvres in 1870. In 1885, the firm was moved to Clichy. During the Art Nouveau period, Sèvres produced a line of acid cut-back cameo floral and foliate designed glassware. Enameled Art Nouveau floral patterns which resemble the large floral enameled glassware produced by Moser, such as the signed example shown in Plate 241, were also produced. Sèvres glassware is a comparative rarity to the American collector; however, when unsigned examples of the type pictured do occur, they can be misattributed as Moser products.

Legras & Cie (France)

Legras & Cie is numbered among the finest French firms which produced Art Nouveau glassware. Founded in 1864 by August-Jean-François Legras, the firm was moved to Pantin in 1897. During the Art Nouveau period, Legras produced a line of cameo glass (Plate 239) with floral decorations under the trademark "Mont Joye." Generally, this glassware is characterized by the use of frosted surfaces on a clear crystal body, considerable gilding, and a pastel enameled floral design (Plate 240). Legras also produced a less costly line of enameled glassware which featured colorful floral patterns on simply shaped crystal. Although large floral enameled glassware produced by Moser resembles the Mont Joye

produce line, differentiating between the products of these two firms should not be difficult. In contrast to the clear crystal blanks employed for the majority of Mont Joye glassware, Moser floral enameling is generally applied to Bohemian type shaded blanks with vertically molded paneling.

Theresienthal

In 1830, King Ludwig of Bavaria requested that the businessman Franz Ludwig Steigerwald build a glasshouse in the Bayr Wald outside of Munich (Germany). Known as Theresienthal, Steigerwald's enterprise was responsible for artistic glass styles which closely resemble those produced by Bohemian and Silesian glasshouses. Until recently, much glassware produced by Theresienthal has been misattributed to the firms of Fritz Heckert and Meyr's Neffe. Plates 243 and 244 illustrate two Theresienthal products which feature naturalistic forms combined with stylized floral patterns. This combination of elements was also employed by Moser enamelists during the latter quarter of the 19th century.

Philippe-Joseph Brocard (France)

Brocard (died 1896) is considered one of the most innovative and talented artists ever to concentrate on the enameled decoration of glass. Initially, Brocard produced enameled mosque lamps which were so in keeping with the originals that experts were required to determine which examples were genuine. Brocard produced a wide diversity of enameled designs based on German and Italian Renaissance and later Gallé inspired Art Nouveau naturalistic themes. He was best known, however, for his renditions of Islamic decorative styles. Although glassware produced by Brocard is rarely available on the open market, examples executed in the Islamic style, typified by the heavily gilded wine goblet in Plate 238, could easily be misrepresented as products of the Moser firm.

IX. Factory Marks

Through the years, Moser signatures have appeared in various guises. Many of the older factory marks persisted alongside newer varieties, so that associating manufacturing dates with specific signatures can often prove misleading. A common thread linking the entire span of Moser production is a script signature (Fig. 86) which ostensibly represents Ludwig Moser's personal signature. Appearing singularly or in combination with "Karlsbad" or "Karlovy Vary," this signature is the one most often encountered by American collectors. In its singular form (i.e., without a town name), the Moser signature is small in size, typically found nestled among the decorative elements of a particular example and is generally difficult to isolate. It is considerably less common to find the singular script "Moser" signature on the base of an item than incorporated within the decorative motif.

For several years, the validity of the singular script Moser signature had been seriously questioned. Since this signature was generally scribed into the glass with a sharp instrument, the addition of spurious signatures by unscrupulous people would be comparatively simple. However, the important question to be answered is whether this particular signature form was actually employed by the Moser factory in the first place.

In arriving at a final conclusion, several factors must be considered. First, if the initial purpose of introducing the script signature was to defraud, why place it within the decorative motif to obscure its presence? Second, within the authors' experience, few articles have been observed bearing the script signature which by themselves would not have been classified as Moser type. Third, several examples have been found which simultaneously bear the script signature and their original paper labels. Fourth, the validity and factory use of the script Moser signature has been confirmed by the Moser family. Finally, the cup and saucer in Plate 60 bear a facsimile of the diamond scribed "Moser" signature applied with a deep acid etching (this is an authentic Moser signature).

Predominantly applied to glass articles during the 1895–1918 time frame, the signature illustrated in Fig. 93 was adopted as the official trademark of the Moser firm and can be found on its business cards and catalogs. An addition of two capital M's separated by a Hock glass to the form in Fig. 93 probably occurred when the Meierhöfen works opened in 1893–1895. Figuratively, this addition signifies the marriage of Ludwig Moser to Julie Meyer and, hence, the joining of two major Bohemian glassmaking families, Moser and Meyer.

While searching the Moser factory records we came across a series of circular trademarks relating to Meyr's Neffe. The first of these, Fig. 78, was employed prior to 1918, while the second, Fig. 79, was probably used in the interim period of 1918 to 1922. Figure 80 appears to be a series of design samples under consideration after

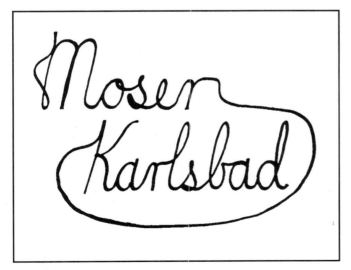

Fig. 76 Broad or fine-line, acid-etched signature; also found in enamel or diamond point scribed. Estimated dates of use are 1870–1925.

Fig. 77 Acid-etched signature; estimated dates of use are 1918–1922.

Figs. 78, 79 and 80 (a,b,c & d). *Above:* Design for Meyr's Neffe trademark used prior to 1918; design for Meyr's Neffe trademark, estimated dates 1918–1922. *Below:* Four Meyr's Neffe trademark designs for use after 1922.

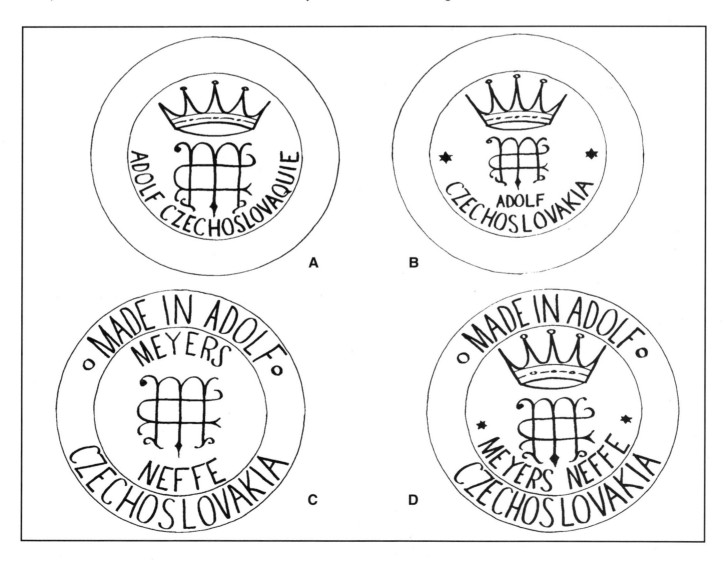

Moser purchased the Adolf glassworks in 1922; Fig. 80d was bracketed in the factory notes and may represent the design finally accepted for commercial use.

We can be certain that the paper label in Fig. 82 was employed as well, as it has been found on the free-blown Alexandrit bottle which also bears the acid-etched signature in Figure 92. Figure 95 illustrates an important paper label employed by Moser prior to 1895. Of particular interest is the spelling of Karlsbad with an English "C" in place of the German "K." Articles bearing this label were probably manufactured for English or American export. Although signed Moser glass predating 1895 is comparatively rare, it is highly probable that most glass marketed before 1895 bore paper labels of this type.

Occasionally, one finds gilded, engraved or enameled numerals on the base of Moser glass. A series of gilded numbers was typically used to designate the basic glass form. These "form numbers" are found alone or in combination with a series of numerals which identify the decorative pattern, i.e., a series of the form 2716/213, designates glass form #2716 and decorative pattern #213. During the production run of similar items requiring custom-fitted stoppers, the stoppers and base (or inside of the lip) were often marked with identical one- or two-digit numbers to ensure proper matching of components. Additional numbers, apparently not falling into either of the above categories, are sometimes found; their purpose was probably to identify specific decorators. Use of form numbers to estimate the earliest production date of a particular item does not appear to be reliable. Research indicates that differing numerical series were employed prior to and after the opening of the Meierhöfen facility.

Contemporary Czech authorities have stated that glassware enameled by Moser was often signed and that the signature was applied using enamels employed during the decorating process; page 90 of Truitt's book on *Collectible Bohemian Glass* illustrates a signature of this type. With regards to Moser glassware found in the

Figs. 81, 82 and 83 *Above left:* Paper label employed after approximately 1925. *Left:* Paper label employed after approximately 1922. *Above:* Acid-etched Wiener Werkstätte/Moser signature employed after 1922.

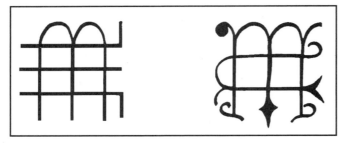

Fig. 84 Comparison of signatures found on products of Lobmeyr and Meyr's Neffe. *Left:* common Lobmeyr signature in gold, enamel or engraved; used after 1860. *Right:* monogram employed by Meyr's Neffe.

Fig. 85 Gilded signature in block letters; estimated dates of use are 1870–1925.

Fig. 86 Singular script signature generally found incorporated within the design elements of a signed example; inscribed with a diamond tipped instrument. Singular signature can also be found enameled (rare) or inscribed with a deep acid etch (also rare). Dates of use cover pre-1870 to approximately 1938.

Fig. 87 Disconnected signature reproduced with acid, enamel or diamond-point inscription. Estimated dates of use are 1870–1925. Karlsbad replaced by Karlovy Vary after approximately 1925.

Figs. 88 and 89 *Above:* Gilded signature in block letters; estimated dates of use are 1870–1895. *Right:* Fine acid-etched signature appearing on items designated for export; estimated dates of use were 1891–1895.

Fig. 90 Diamond point scribed signature occurring with or without "Made in." Separation of Czecho and Slovakia in signature dates from 1918 to approximately 1922; name joined as Czechoslovakia after that date. Karlsbad was used in signature up to approximately 1925; Karlovy Vary was used after that date.

Fig. 91 Acid-etched signature designating Heinrich Haussman designed glassware, c. 1930.

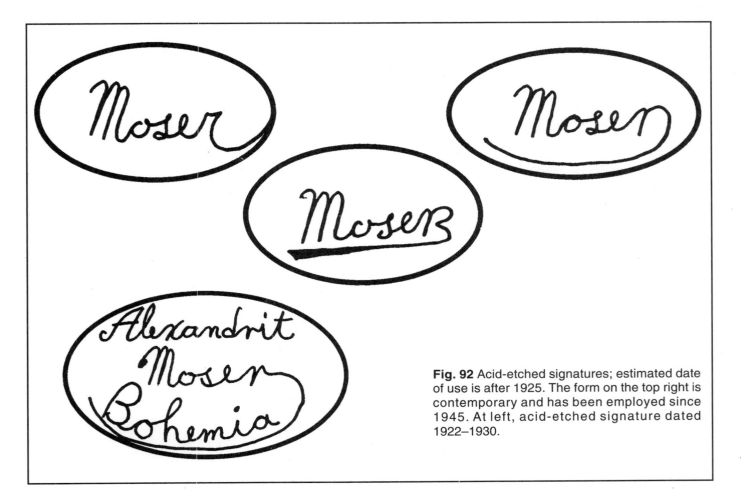

Fig. 92 Acid-etched signatures; estimated date of use is after 1925. The form on the top right is contemporary and has been employed since 1945. At left, acid-etched signature dated 1922–1930.

Fig. 93 Fine acid-etched Moser trademark used from approximately 1895 to 1938; items designated for export incorporate "Made in Austria" prior to 1819 and "Made in Czechoslovakia" after 1819. Primary use as a signature on glass was in the 1895–1918 time frame.

Figs. 94 and 95 *Above left:* Cameo signature primarily found on "Animor" series glassware. *Above:* Export paper label emblazoned with the Hapsburg Eagle; primarily employed prior to 1890.

Fig. 96 *Left:* Meyr's Neffe paper label employed after 1922.

United States, the type of signature illustrated in Truitt's book is extremely rare. Furthermore, the form of the "Moser" signature is totally different from the normal forms given in Fig. 86. This signature may have been common to glassware retained for Central European consumption, but was not common to glassware exported to the United States. The conclusion that Moser glassware is often marked is reasonably accurate for glassware produced after WWI. Prior to WWII, however, the majority of Moser glass was not indelibly signed.

As has been mentioned previously, this chapter closes with a word of warning concerning the reliance on a signature to establish a Moser attribution. Fraudulent Moser signatures, encompassing both the scribed and acid-etched forms, are an ever present reality. Many of the examples bearing fraudulent signatures were actually marketed by the Moser firm, while others, primarily exhibiting poor quality workmanship, are of diverse origin. This problem is compounded by the fact that a multiplicity of signature forms were employed by the Moser firm and that new types are constantly being discovered. Signatures included in this book are of a more common variety but by no means represent a complete listing. It cannot be overemphasized that recognition of artistic and technical quality, in addition to a basic knowledge of the glass styles produced by a specific manufacturer, is of paramount important in purchasing artistic glass. Absolute reliance on the presence of a signature can prove quite disappointing from both an aesthetic as well as a financial point of view.

X. Moser—A Summary of Excellence

Within a comparatively short period, the firm founded by Ludwig Moser ascended from the drab surroundings of a spa engraving studio to become a world celebrated supplier of artistic glass. Through an international network of fine shops, Ludwig Moser sold luxury glassware to socially prominent and wealthy patrons. Included among his customers were many of the crowned heads in Europe and the Middle East. Even though Ludwig Moser was recognized by his contemporaries as a painter and engraver of significant stature, his greatest achievement was as a glassmaker. The Moser firm's unparalleled success was the direct result of Ludwig's personal dedication to the production of glassware of uncompromising quality.

During the period between 1857 and 1895, glass marketed by Moser consisted of highly distinctive decorative motifs applied to glass blanks purchased from major Bohemian glasshouses. Success abroad was ensured by an extensive network of glass merchandising centers. At home, the appointment of Ludwig Moser as "Supplier of Glass" to the Austrian Imperial Court of Franz Joseph solidified his position as a major Bohemian manufacturer of artistic glass.

1895 witnessed the completion of Moser's glassworks at Meierhöfen and with it a major shift in emphasis away from the production of intricately enameled glassware. Technical perfection of the glass melt and forming process, development of complementary cutting and engraving techniques and the introduction of new colored glass formulations became an all-consuming passion. Such dedication to excellence was rewarded by a high level of visibility at international competitions and a seemingly endless procession of socially prominent patrons.

In 1922, the Moser firm, under the artistic directorship of Leo Moser, purchased Meyr's Neffe's Adolf works in southern Bohemia. Although Moser produced decorative glassware designed by the noted Art Deco artist Joseph Hoffman prior to World War I, the acquisition of Meyr's Neffe opened the door to the full design capability of the Wiener Werkstätte association of artists. Beginning around 1875, Meyr's Neffe had been the major supplier of enameled glass to the celebrated firm of J. & L. Lobmeyr. After the merger, Moser lost little time in capitalizing on this expertise. As a result of the combined design and artistic resources of the two firms, enameled glassware marketed by Moser, regained—and in some aspects surpassed—its former splendor.

At Meierhöfen, Leo Moser continued the development of richly colored glasses and, in 1922, was the first to introduce commercial production of rare-earth doped glasses. Advanced prismatic cutting styles designed to enhance the jewel-like properties of these new glasses won international acclaim. These achievements, in combination with the fact that glass cutters and engravers retained by the Moser firm were recognized as among the finest available in Central Europe, attracted the attention of locally and internationally prominent glass artists and designers. During the 1920s, Moser became a forum of contemporary design. Uniquely designed glassware, representing a significant departure from traditional Moser product lines, was commissioned in quantity and, in many instances, found its way into international competitions. Artistic glass produced by the Moser firm during the two decades following World War I reached a pinnacle of design and technical execution which remains unsurpassed up to the present day.

Fortunately, World War II left the Moser factory at Meierhöfen unscathed and it took little time for the Czech government to reestablish Moser as one of Czechoslovakia's leading glasshouses. Under Communism, the international reputation of Moser suffered from political censorship and the inability of merchandisers to reliably obtain Moser glass for their showrooms. Since the fall of Communism and the re-establishment of a free enterprise economy, Moser is striving to regain its former international presence. Firm reliance on the popularity and social acceptance of designs produced prior to World War II, as well as a progressive look to the future through the eyes of contemporary Czech artists, has once more established Moser as the dominant producer of luxury glass in Central Europe.

THE SEARCH CONTINUES

In presenting the material contained within these pages the author has tried to be as factual as possible. In some cases, however, conclusions drawn reflect the blending of documented evidence with deductive reasoning. Historical accounts were largely assembled from published information and, as such, are dependent on the original material for their accuracy. Records brought to the United States by Leo Moser can be considered "firsthand" information. But, here also, notes concerning the history of the Moser firm prior to 1916 were not contemporary with their occurrence and are consequently subject to lapses in memory.

A large portion of the glass samples presented in this book are of a type readily available to the American collector. In some cases a Moser attribution is based on the often fraudulent "Moser" script signature. For others, the attribution is based on the similarity of decorative patterns and techniques to documented Moser examples. It is interesting to note that given Moser's penchant for catering to specialized geographical markets, many of these articles may well be considered rare in certain parts of the world.

Following in the footsteps of *Moser—Artistry in Glass*, this book represents a second step in assembling a comprehensive body of information concerning the history and artistic output of the Moser firm. As before, many gray areas still exist, and it is to these subjects that we must continue to address our investigative efforts. Past geopolitical conditions, the diversity in design exhibited by Moser products, and the existence of similar glassware marketed by rival firms severely complicate the gathering of definitive information. Factory catalogs or sales brochures issued by branch offices, such as those which were established in New York (USA), represent a valuable source of information; unfortunately, the existence of such items or their whereabouts remains an open question.

With the establishment of the Czech Republic, sources of information previously inaccessible to Western researchers hold the promise of substantially increasing our knowledge of Bohemian glass production. Although, at present, it appears that the bulk of existing Moser factory records are represented by the documentation brought to this country by Leo Moser, additional historical and product information on Moser may be uncovered from the records of firms with which Moser had business ties. Meyr's Neffe's factory records, for example, could throw substantial light on the enameled glassware produced from 1922 to 1933 and probably increase our knowledge of the Modern and Art Deco glassware styles produced by Moser.

In the face of limited documentation, collectors, as well as knowledgeable antique dealers represent a valuable information resource. An appeal goes out to these individuals that any new or controversial information, no matter how small or seemingly insignificant, be brought to the author's attention.

One final thought: let glass historians sift through dusty archives and argue over the authenticity of this and that. At best, such activities represent but a complementary diversion from the real significance of artistic glass. At once a unique harmonization of function and aesthetic appear, fine glass is a lofty expression of artistic ideals which entreats those who possess it to sit back, relax and enjoy.

Town Cross-Reference Table

CZECH NAME	GERMAN NAME
Albrechtice	Albrechtsdorf
Česká Lípa	Böhmisch Leipa
Cheb	Eger
Cieplice	Warmbrunn
Dvory (part of Karlovy Vary)	Meierhöfen
Františkovy Lázně	Franzensbad
Harrachov	Harrachsdorf
Jablonec	Gablonz
Kamênický Šenov	Steinschönau
Karlovy Vary	Karlsbad
Klášterský Mlýn	Klostermühle
Koštány	Kosten
Lenora	Eleonorenhain
Liberec	Reichenberg
Mariánské Láznê	Marienbad
Mistrovice	Meistersdorf
Nový Bor	Haida
Nový Svêt	Neuwelt
Piechowice	Petersdorf
Poděbrady	Podebrad
Polubný	Polaun
Praha	Prag (English, Prague)
Skalice u České Lípy	Langenau
Sklarzska Poreba	Schrieberhau
Sloup	Röhrsdorf
Teplice	Teplitz-Schönau
Vimperk	Winterberg
Zákupy	Reichstadt
Železný Brod	Eisenbrod

Index

Bibliography

Adressbuch Europas Glasindustrie. Herausgegeben von der Redaktion der Zeilschrift: "Die Glashütte." Dresden, 1925.

Arwas, Victor. *Glass Art Nouveau to Art Deco.* New York: Rizzoli International Publishing Inc., 1980.

Blau, Josef. *Die Glasmacher in Böhmer-und Bayerwald.* Regensburg: im Verlag Michael Lassleben Kallmunz, 1956.

Bloch-Dermant, Janine. *The Art of French Glass, 1860–1914.* New York: The Vendome Press, 1974.

Bohemian Glass, 1400–1989. New York: Harry N. Abrams, Inc., 1990.

Bohemian Glass, Tradition and...Present. Crystalex: Nový Bor, 1991.

Brohan, Sammlung Karl H. "Kunsthandwerk-Glas Holz Keramik." Berlin, 1976.

Buckley, W. *European Glass.* New York: Houghton Mifflin Co., 1926.

Campana, D. M. "Enamel Decorations for Porcelain and Glass." *Campana's Popular Art Library*, 2nd ed., 1947.

Ćeskísklo, *XIX stoleti*, Moravska Galerie V. Brnê, Ĉerven-Źaî, 1979.

Charon, Mural K. *Ludwig (Ludvik) Moser—King of Glass.* Hillsdale, Michigan: Charon/Ferguson–Division of Ferguson Communications, 1984.

Corning Museum of Glass. *Czechoslovakian Glass.* New York: Dover Publications, 1981.

Cox, Claude V. *Ludwig Moser—Royal Glass Artisan.* Decatur, Illinois: Coxes Collectables, 1978.

Crystalex Branch Corporation. *Bohemian Glass.* Nový Bor: 1985.

Curtis, Jean-Louis. *Baccarat.* New York: Harry N. Abrams, Inc., 1992.

"Das Böhmische Glas, 1700–1905." Herausgeber, Georg Höltl. Passauer Glasmuseum, 1996.

Davis, Frank. *Antique Glass and Glass Collecting.* London: Hamlyn Publishing Group, Ltd., 1973.

Drahotova, Olga. *European Art Glass.* New York: Excalibur Books, 1983.

Fahdt, Julius. *Die Glasindustrie Oesterreich-Ungarns.* Dresden: Selbstverlag, 1901.

Feller, John Quentin. "Katharine Louise Dorflinger: Christian Dorflinger's Daughter and Heir," *The National Early American Glass Club Bulletin*, No. 148 (Winter 1985–86).

Garner, Philippe, ed. *The Encyclopedia of Decorative Arts.* New York: Van Nostrand Reinhold Co., 1979.

Gilard, P., et al. "The Fluorescence of Glass," *The Glass Industry.* New York: March 1938.

"Glas, Historismus und die Historismen um 1900." Staatliche Musee zu Berlin, Kunstgewerbemuseum Schlob Köpenick, Nov. 1977.

"Glass," *Smithsonian Illustrated Library of Antiques.* Prepared by the Cooper-Hewitt Museum, 1979.

"Glass of 5 Centuries." Glass Gallery Michael Kovacek. Vienna: Michael Kovacek, 1990.

"Glass of 5 Centuries." Glasgalerie Michael Kovacek. Vienna: Michael Kovacek, 1993.

Gros-Galliner, Gabriella. *Glass, A Guide for Collectors.* New York: Stein and Day Publishers, 1970.

Grover, Lee and Ray. *Art Glass Nouveau.* Rutland, Vermont: Charles E. Tuttle Co., 1967.

Grover, Lee and Ray. *European Art Glass*. Rutland, Vermont: Charles E. Tuttle Co., 1970.

Gruber, Sammlung H. R. "Jugend stilglas." Mainz: Mittelrheinisches Landesnaseum, 1976.

Gysling-Billeter, Erika. *Objekte des jugendstils*. Bem: Benteli Verlag, 1975.

Hájek, Jindřich. "Karlovy Vary—The Cradle of the 'Glass of Kings.'" *Czech. Glass Review*, Vol. 2 (1964), 42.

Heacock, Bill. *Collecting Glass*, Vol. 1. Marietta, Ohio: Antique Publications, 1985.

Hilschenz, Helga. "Das Glas des Jugendstils." Katalog der Sammlung Heutrich im Kunstmuseum Dusseldorf, Prestel-Verlag. München, 1973.

"Historismus—Kunsthandwerk und industrie im Zeitalter der Weltausstellungen," Staatliche Museen, Preussischer Kulturbesitz.

Jargstorf, Sibylle. *Baubles, Buttons and Beads, The Heritage of Bohemia*. Atglen, Pennsylvania: Schiffer Publishing. Co., 1993.

"Katalog der Kunstgewerbemuseums," Berlin Bd. VII. Berlin, 1973.

Kreidl, Norbert J. "Rare Earths," *Journal of the American Ceramic Society*, Vol. 25 (1942), 141–143.

Kutac, Vincene. "120 Years of Existence of the Moser Glassworks at Karlovy Vary," *Czech. Glass Review*, Vol. 32 (1977), 2–6.

Langhamer, Antonín. "Engraved Glass from the Karlovarske Sklo Glassworks," *Czech. Glass Review*, Vol. 32 (1977), 7–11.

"Leerdam Unica." 50 Jahre Modernes Niederldndisches Glas, Kunstmuseum Dusseldorf, 1977. Museum Boymans-van Beuningen Rotterdam, 1977.

Mackay, James. *Dictionary of Turn of the Century Antiques*. London: Wardlock Limited, 1974.

Manley, Cyril. *Decorative Victorian Glass*. New York: Van Nostrand Reinhold, 1981.

Matura, Adolf. "Moser Karlovy Vary Glass," *Czech. Glass Review*, June 1964, 163–169.

McClinton, Katherine Morrison. *Art Deco—A Guide for Collectors*. New York: Clarkson N. Potter, Inc., 1972.

McKearin, George S. and Helen. *American Glass*. New York: Crown Publishers, 1946.

Middlemas, Keith. *Antique Glass in Color*. New York: Doubleday and Co., 1971.

Moser, Leo. "Commercial Art Glass," *The Glass Industry*. New York: March 1942.

Mundt, Barbara. *Historismus*. Berlin, 1974.

Mundt, Barbara. *Historismus*. München: Keysersche Verlagsbuchhandlung, 1981.

Neuwirth, Waltraud. "Glas, 1905–1925, Band 1." Wein: Selbstverlag Dr. Waltraud Neuwirth, 1985.

Neuwirth, Waltraud. "Löetz Austria 1900." Wein: Selbstverlag Dr. Waltraud Neuwirth, 1986.

Neuwirth, Waltraud. "Löetz, Austria 1905–1918." Wein: Selbstverlag Dr. Waltraud Neuwirth, 1986.

Neuwirth, Waltraud. *Orientalisierende Glaser, J. & L. Lobmeyr, Band 1*. Wien: Selbstverlag Dr. Waltraud Neuwirth, 1981.

Neuwirth, Waltraud. *Wiener Werkstätte*. Wien: Selbstverlag Dr. Waltraud Neuwirth, 1984.

Newman, Harold. *An Illustrated Dictionary of Glass*. London: Thames and Hudson Ltd., 1977.

Pazaurek, Gustav E. *Glaser der Empire—und Biedermeierzeit*. Klinkhardt und Biermann.

Pazaurek, Gustav E. *Modern Glaser*. Leipzig: Hermann Seemann Nachfoldge, 1910.

Pazaurek, Gustav E., and Walter Spiegl. *Glas des 20. Jahrhunderts, Jugendstil-Art Déco*. Munchen: Klinkhardt & Biermann, 1983.

Pesatova, Zuzana. *Bohemian Engraved Glass*. Prague: Knihtisk, 1968.

Phillips, Phoebe. *The Encyclopedia of Glass*. New York: Crown Publishers, Inc., 1981.

Polak, Ada. *Glass—Its Tradition and its Makers*. New York: G. P. Putnam's Sons, 1975.

Revi, Albert Christian. *Nineteenth Century Glass*. New York: Galahad Books, 1959/1967.

Riedel Since 1756—10 Generations of Glassmakers. Museum of Glass and Bijouterie in Jablonec n.N. Gablonz, 19 August–27 Oct., 1991

Ricke, Helmut. "Böhmisches Glass 1880–1940, Band 1, Wermonographie." Also "Band 2, Katalog der Musterschnitte" (two volumes). Prestel, Müchen/New York, 1989.

Robertson, R. A. *Chat on Old Glass*. New York: Dover Publications, Inc., 1969.

Savage, George. *Glass and Glassware*. London: Octopus Books Ltd., 1973.

Schmidt, Robert. *Lobmeyer, 1823–1923*. Wien: Anton Schroll & Co.

Schuman, John A. III. *Art Glass Sampler*. Des Moines, Iowa: Wallace-Homestead, 1978.

Schweiger, Werner J. *Wiener Werkstätte—Design in Vienna, 1902–1932*. New York: Abbeville Press, 1984.

Spiegl, Walter. *Glas des Historismus*. Braunschweig: Klinkhardt & Biermann, 1980.

"The 125th Anniversary of the Moser Glassworks at Karlovy Vary," *Czech. Glass Review*, Vol. 36 (1981), 2–28.

Truitt, Robert and Deborah. *Collectible Bohemian Glass, 1880–1940*. Kensington, Maryland: B & D Glass, 1995.

Villain, Jean. "The History of the Bohemian Glass Blowers." Weltbuehne, Ost Berlin, March 1960.

Vose, Ruth Hurst. *Glass*. London: The Connoisseur, 1975.

Vratislav, Sotolam. "Nekonvencní Moser," *Domov*, No. 6 (1966), 16–19.

Warthorst, Karl-Wilhelm. *Die Glasfabrik Theresienthal*. Dr. Neuner Verlag: 1996.

Weiss, Gustav. *The Book of Glass*. Praeger Publishing Co., 1971.

Weyl, Woldemart. *Colored Glass*. Sheffield, England: Society of Glass Technology.

Zimmerman. "Hollandisches Glas, Glaser von Chris Lebeau," *Die Schaulade*. 1928.

Moser Artistic Glass
Edition Two

1997–1998 RETAIL PRICE GUIDE

Pricing hand-worked artistic glass of the type marketed by Moser and other glasshouses represents a difficult task. Part of the problem arises from the almost endless variety of unique artistic styles produced. Each separate example must be evaluated as to its overall artistic design, quality of execution, physical condition, rarity and the presence or lack of an authentic signature. Market demand, which is largely regional, and the cost of doing business further influence the price a dealer might place on a specific item. If one considers contemporary manufacturing costs, Moser glass is largely undervalued in today's market. While this is certainly good news from an investment standpoint, it does increase the probability of finding examples priced at significantly higher values than estimates quoted in this book.

In preparing the following price guide, the author has standardized on a range of *retail* prices which would most likely be charged by an antique or art dealer knowledgeable in the field. Several items in this book fall under the categories of museum pieces; or represent stylistic forms which rarely occur on the open market; or are examples of contemporary Moser products which are available from either the Moser factory or retail outlets in the United States and Europe. No price information will be provided for articles falling into these three categories, and each item is designated by "N/P" (for no price). Since value placed on signed examples is largely subjective and, in the author's opinion, should not significantly influence asking price, prices quoted reflect artistic value independent of the presence or lack of an authentic signature. Neither the author nor the publisher can be held liable for losses incurred when using this price guide as the basis for any transaction.

Values given are for undamaged examples. When gilding is encountered, moderate wear, especially on lip rims, is generally acceptable; however, heavy loss of gold should significantly reduce market value.

Plate No.	Description	Est. Price Range
1	Disassembled Zwischengoldglas tumbler	$ N/P
2	Biedermeier Annegrün tankard	1200 – 1500
3	Pitcher *(left)*	350 – 450
"	Covered box *(center)*	450 – 550
"	Pitcher *(right)*	800 – 1000
4	Partial garniture set	N/P
5	Cameo and intaglio engraved vase	4000 – 5000
6	Punch set (seven cups)	3500 – 4500
7	Enameled and gilded urns (price for each)	1200 – 1400
8	Portrait vases (*left and right*; price for each)	400 – 600
"	Portrait vase *(center)*	1800 – 2200
9	Portrait vase	1200 – 1500
10	Decanter *(center)*	1400 – 1600
"	Goblets (each)	450 – 550
11	Flower-form vase	2500 – 3000
12	Fish vase *(left)*	1500 – 1800
"	Pokal *(center)*	2000 – 2300
"	Cat vase *(right)*	1800 – 2100
13	Fern-leaf vase	2500 – 3000
14	Master salt *(left)*	450 – 650
"	Sugar and creamer (set)	900 – 1100
15	Rubina ewer	1200 – 1500
16	Pitcher *(left)*	400 – 500
"	Finger bowl and underplate *(center)*	700 – 800
"	Mug *(right)*	500 – 600
17	Casket *(left)*	1200 – 1400
"	Casket *(right)*	1600 – 1800
18	Fern-leaf vase (price for each)	1500 – 1800
19	Goblet *(left)*	500 – 700
"	Vase *(center)*	500 – 700
"	Goblet *(right)*	800 – 1100
20	Jeweled tumbler	500 – 700
21	Decanter *(left)*	800 – 1200
"	Cup and saucer *(center)*	400 – 600
"	Decanter *(right)*	1800 – 2200
22	Charger	3000 – 3500
23	Iridescent vase	400 – 500

PLATE NO.	DESCRIPTION	EST. PRICE RANGE
24	Decanter	$1500 – 1800
25	Flower-form vase	1800 – 2200
26	Wine goblet	1700 – 1900
27	Vase *(left)*	400 – 500
"	Vase *(right)*	900 – 1200
28	Tri-footed rose bowl	3800 – 4000
29	Pitcher	4500 – 5000
30	Tree-form tazza	3500 – 3800
31	See above	
32	Chalice	2200 – 2500
33	Ewer	1200 –1500
34	Bowl	6000 – 8000
35	See above	
36	Pitcher	2800 – 3200
37	Beaker	1800 – 2200
38	Footed bowl	1500 – 1800
39	Hunting mug	900 – 1200
40	Atomizer	700 – 900
41	Loving cup	1800 – 2200
42	Vases *(left and center*; price for each)	1200 – 1500
"	Pitcher *(right)*	800 – 1000
43	Vase with salamander *(upper left)*	3400 – 3600
"	Vases *(upper right*; price for each)	1500 – 1800
"	Mug *(lower left)*	1800 – 2200
"	Vase *(lower right)*	2500 – 2800
44	Robin vase	2000 – 2300
45	Eagle vase	4200 – 4500
46	Mold-blown vase	800 – 1200
47	Vases (price for each)	4000 – 4500
48	Pitcher *(lower left)*	350 – 450
"	Vase *(upper right)*	600 – 800
"	Vase *(lower right)*	250 – 350
49	Jeweled vase	2800 – 3200
50	Vase *(left)*	600 – 800
"	Cologne *(center)*	1000 – 1200
"	Vase *(right)*	500 – 700
51	Charger	2200 – 2500

PLATE NO.	DESCRIPTION	EST. PRICE RANGE
52	Vase	$1200 – 1500
53	Bowl	1500 – 1800
54	Cordials (price for each)	350 – 450
55	Vase	2500 – 2800
56	Creamer (left)	800 – 1200
"	Sugar and creamer (center)	1200 – 1500
"	Pokal (left)	1800 – 2200
57	Covered bowl (left)	600 – 800
"	Miniature covered bowl (left of center)	350 – 450
"	Cornucopia vase (right of center)	600 – 800
"	Creamer (right)	700 – 900
58	Decanter (left)	600 – 800
"	Pitcher (center)	1200 – 1500
"	Vase (right)	600 – 800
59	Pokal	3500 – 3800
60	Decanter (left)	800 – 1200
"	Cup and saucer (left of center)	400 – 500
"	Creamer (center)	300 – 400
"	Vase (right of center)	400 – 600
"	Champagne flute (right)	350 – 450
61	Chalice (left)	800 – 1200
"	Chalice (right)	800 – 1200
62	Sugar shaker	1200 – 1500
63	Vase (left)	900 – 1100
"	Vase (center)	500 – 700
"	Vase (right)	700 – 900
64	Decanter (priced complete with stopper)	1800 – 2200
65	Mary Gregory style vase	900 – 1200
66	Ewer (left)	250 – 350
"	Obelisk (right)	500 – 700
67	Water set	2500 – 2800
68	Mounted bowl	1500 – 1800
69	Vase	2500 – 2800
70	Donut ewer	1500 – 1800
71	Large rose bowl (left and right; price for each)	500 – 700
"	Small rose bowl (center)	350 – 450
72	Small wine (top row, left)	225 – 275

Plate No.	Description	Est. Price Range
72	Decanter *(top row, right)*	$ 900 – 1200
"	Tumbler *(2nd row, left)*	175 – 225
"	Cordial *(2nd row, left of center)*	90 – 110
"	Juice glass *(2nd row, right of center)*	125 – 150
"	Finger bowl and underplate *(2nd row, right)*	400 – 500
"	Champagne *(3rd row, left)*	250 – 300
"	Wine *(3rd row, left of center)*	450 – 550
"	Water *(3rd row, right of center)*	300 – 350
"	Cordial decanter *(3rd row, right)*	800 – 1000
73	Decanter set	1500 – 1800
74	Salts *(left; price for each)*	250 – 350
"	Lidded box	300 – 400
75	Vase *(top left)*	200 – 250
"	Miniature stein *(top right)*	800 – 1200
"	Mounted vase *(top center)*	250 – 350
"	Creamer *(lower left)*	250 – 350
"	Creamer *(lower right)*	200 – 300
"	Vase *(lower center)*	400 – 500
76	Tumble-up	800 – 1200
77	Water pitcher	1200 – 1500
78	Rubina pitcher	2800 – 3200
79	Water goblet	500 – 700
80	Decanter set (two goblets; *left*)	1000 – 1200
"	Decanter set (six cordials; *right*)	1200 – 1500
81	Vases *(left and right*; price for each)	500 – 700
"	Vase *(center)*	500 – 700
82	Humidor	1800 – 2200
83	Vase	1200 – 1500
84	Decanter set (with two goblets)	1200 – 1500
85	Domed box *(upper left)*	450 – 550
"	Domed box *(upper right)*	400 – 500
"	Domed box *(lower left)*	350 – 450
"	Domed box *(lower right)*	600 – 700
86	Vases *(left and right*; price for each)	600 – 800
"	Stirrup cup *(center)*	350 – 450
87	Engraved vase	350 – 450
88	Decanter set (with two cups)	800 – 1200

PLATE NO.	DESCRIPTION	EST. PRICE RANGE
89	Decanter set (with six cordials)	$1500 – 1800
90	Iridescent bowl	800 – 1000
91	Vase	500 – 600
92	Vase	450 – 550
93	Vase *(left)*	450 – 550
"	Vase *(center)*	450 – 550
"	Vase *(right)*	300 – 400
94	Römers *(left*; price for each)	350 – 450
"	Covered box	550 – 650
95	Footed plate *(left)*	1500 – 1800
"	Plate *(center)*	350 – 450
"	Wine goblet *(right)*	300 – 350
96	Decanter set (with five cordials)	2500 – 3000
97	Mounted vase	1200 – 1500
98	Pokal	3200 – 3400
99	Vase *(left)*	500 – 600
"	Vase *(center)*	450 – 550
"	Vase *(right)*	600 – 700
100	Covered bowl	800 – 1000
101	Flask *(left)*	450 – 550
" "	Sherbet and underplate *(center)*	350 – 450
" "	Cologne *(top right)*	550 – 650
" "	Cup and saucer *(bottom right)*	300 – 400
102	Decanter *(left)*	1000 – 1200
" "	Footed vase *(right)*	1200 – 1500
103	Vases (price for each)	3800 – 4200
104	Wine goblets, *top row*	
" "	1st from left	350 – 450
" "	2nd from left	450 – 550
" "	3rd from left	350 – 450
" "	4th from left	350 – 450
" "	5th from left	800 – 1000
" "	6th from left	400 – 500
" "	7th from left	350 – 450
" "	Wine goblets, *middle row*	
" "	1st from left	450 – 550
" "	2nd from left	450 – 550

Plate No.	Description	Est. Price Range
104	3rd from left	$ 500 – 600
" "	4th from left	350 – 450
" "	5th from left	250 – 350
" "	6th from left	350 – 450
" "	7th from left	350 – 450
" "	Wine goblets, *bottom row*	
" "	1st from left	350 – 450
" "	2nd from left	250 – 350
" "	3rd from left	450 – 550
" "	4th from left	550 – 650
" "	5th from left	600 – 700
" "	6th from left	350 – 450
105	Wine goblets, *top row*	
" "	1st from left	300 – 400
" "	2nd from left	400 – 500
" "	3rd from left	450 – 550
" "	4th from left	700 – 800
" "	5th from left	400 – 500
" "	6th from left	700 – 800
" "	7th from left	250 – 350
" "	Wine goblets, *middle row*	
" "	1st from left	700 – 800
" "	2nd from left	350 – 450
" "	3rd from left	400 – 500
" "	4th from left	450 – 550
" "	5th from left	350 – 450
" "	6th from left	600 – 700
" "	7th from left	700 – 800
" "	Wine goblets, *bottom row*	
" "	1st from left	300 – 400
" "	2nd from left	350 – 450
" "	3rd from left	900 – 1100
" "	4th from left	350 – 450
" "	5th from left	700 – 800
" "	6th from left	400 – 500
" "	7th from left	300 – 400

PLATE NO.	DESCRIPTION	EST. PRICE RANGE
106	Juice glasses, *top row*	
" "	1st from left	$ 125 – 150
" "	2nd from left	125 – 150
" "	3rd from left	150 – 200
" "	4th from left	150 – 175
" "	5th from left	125 – 150
" "	6th from left	125 – 150
" "	7th from left	125 – 150
" "	8th from left	250 – 300
" "	Juice glasses, *2nd row*	
" "	1st from left	250 – 300
" "	2nd from left	125 – 150
" "	3rd from left	150 – 200
" "	4th from left	125 – 150
" "	5th from left	400 – 500
" "	6th from left	125 – 150
" "	7th from left	125 – 150
" "	Juice glasses, *3rd row*	
" "	1st from left	125 – 150
" "	2nd from left	150 – 200
" "	3rd from left	125 – 150
" "	4th from left	125 – 150
" "	5th from left	125 – 150
" "	6th from left	125 – 150
" "	7th from left	250 – 300
" "	8th from left	200 – 250
" "	Juice glasses, *4th row*	
" "	1st from left	150 – 200
" "	2nd from left	120 – 150
" "	3rd from left	250 – 300
" "	4th from left	250 – 300
" "	5th from left	250 – 300
" "	6th from left	150 – 200
" "	7th from left	125 – 150
" "	8th from left	125 – 200
" "	Juice glasses, *bottom row*	
" "	1st from left	125 – 150

Plate No.	Description	Est. Price Range
106	2nd from left	$ 125 – 150
" "	3rd from left	125 – 200
107	Juice glasses, *top row*	
" "	1st from left	125 – 150
" "	2nd from left	125 – 150
" "	3rd from left	125 – 150
" "	4th from left	125 – 150
" "	5th from left	150 – 200
" "	6th from left	125 – 150
" "	7th from left	200 – 250
" "	8th from left	300 – 400
" "	Juice glasses, *2nd row*	
" "	1st from left	125 – 150
" "	2nd from left	125 – 150
" "	3rd from left	300 – 350
" "	4th from left	125 – 150
" "	5th from left	125 – 150
" "	6th from left	150 – 200
" "	7th from left	150 – 200
" "	Juice glasses, *3rd row*	
" "	1st from left	125 – 150
" "	2nd from left	125 – 150
" "	3rd from left	250 – 300
" "	4th from left	125 – 150
" "	5th from left	200 – 250
" "	6th from left	120 – 150
" "	7th from left	125 – 150
" "	8th from left	125 – 150
" "	Juice glasses, *4th row*	
" "	1st from left	125 – 150
" "	2nd from left	125 – 150
" "	3rd from left	125 – 150
" "	4th from left	250 – 300
" "	5th from left	250 – 300
" "	6th from left	125 – 150
" "	7th from left	200 – 250
" "	8th from left	125 – 150

Plate No.	Description	Est. Price Range
107	Juice glasses, *bottom row*	
" "	1st from left	$ 125 – 150
" "	2nd from left	300 – 350
" "	3rd from left	125 – 150
108	Decanter	1200 – 1500
109	Decanter set (with six goblets)	1800 – 2200
110	Vase *(left)*	250 – 350
" "	Footed bowl *(center)*	300 – 400
" "	Vase *(right)*	450 – 550
111	Vase *(left)*	700 – 900
" "	Vase *(center)*	400 – 500
" "	Pitcher *(right)*	700 – 800
112	Charger	800 – 1000
113	Vase	500 – 600
114	Sugar and creamer *(left and right)*	500 – 600
" "	Plate *(center)*	350 – 450
115	Sherbet and underplate *(left)*	300 – 400
" "	Goblet *(left)*	300 – 400
116	Cup and saucer *(left)*	350 – 450
" "	Cup and saucer *(center)*	350 – 450
" "	Goblet *(right)*	350 – 450
117	Goblet *(left)*	300 – 400
" "	Goblet *(right)*	300 – 400
118	Decanter *(left)*	400 – 500
" "	Cup and saucer *(right)*	250 – 350
119	Vase	1750 – 2250
120	Engraved vase	2000 – 2500
121	Decanter set (with two cordials)	2500 – 3000
122	Marquetry vase	7000 – 9000
123	Marquetry vase	2500 – 3500
124	Marquetry goblet *(left)*	2000 – 2500
" "	Marquetry goblet *(right)*	1500 – 1800
125	Decanter Set (with four goblets)	3000 – 3500
126	Marquetry vase	1800 – 2200
127	Vase *(left)*	1200 – 1600
" "	Rose bowl *(center)*	400 – 500
" "	Low vase *(right)*	600 – 800

PLATE NO.	DESCRIPTION	EST. PRICE RANGE
128	Diamond-shaped box *(left)*	$ 700 – 900
" "	Vase *(center)*	800 – 1200
" "	Vase *(right)*	600 – 800
129	Three-handled vase	1200 – 1500
130	Cruet	800 – 1200
131	Atomizer *(left)*	400 – 500
" "	Atomizer *(center)*	1200 – 1500
" "	Atomizer *(right)*	500 – 700
132	Moser vase *(left)*	800 – 1200
" "	Harrach vase *(right)*	800 – 1200
133	Cameo vase	3500 – 4500
134	Cameo vase	800 – 1200
135	Karlsbader Secession vase	4500 – 5500
136	Decanter set (with two goblets)	1800 – 2200
137	Vase *(left)*	350 – 450
" "	Bowl *(center)*	500 – 700
" "	Pitcher *(right)*	1200 – 1500
138	Iris vase *(left)*	800 – 1200
" "	Vase *(2nd from left)*	800 – 1200
" "	Vase *(3rd from left)*	600 – 800
" "	Pansy vase *(right)*	800 – 1200
139	Vase *(left)*	1200 – 1500
" "	Vase *(right)*	1400 – 1800
140	Cameo lidded vase	2500 – 3500
141	Vase *(left)*	800 – 1200
" "	Vase *(right)*	600 – 800
142	Cameo decanter set (with six cordials)	1200 – 1800
143	Cameo vase	1200 – 1600
144	Cameo footed bowl	800 – 1200
145	Cameo atomizer	700 – 900
146	Scenic vase	4500 – 5500
147	Chalice *(left)*	2500 – 3500
" "	Juice glass *(center)*	250 – 300
" "	Chalice *(right)*	2500 – 3500
148	Decanter set (with six goblets)	3000 – 4000
149	Jeweled beer glasses *(left and right*; price for each)	800 – 1000
" "	Jeweled beer pitcher *(center)*	3500 – 4500

Plate No.	Description	Est. Price Range
150	Jeweled vase	$1200 – 1600
151	Jeweled vase	1000 – 1500
152	Engraved lidded bowl	1500 – 1800
153	Jeweled tumbler	350 – 450
154	Vase	1500 – 1800
155	Wedding goblet	1200 – 1500
156	Engraved goblet	350 – 450
157	Vase	1200 – 1500
158	Pokal	600 – 800
159	Animor vase *(left)*	3500 – 4000
" "	Animor vase *(right)*	2500 – 3500
160	Masque vase	3500 – 4500
161	Cameo stork vase	2500 – 3000
162	Wine goblet *(left)*	800 – 1200
" "	Wine goblet *(center)*	300 – 400
" "	Wine goblet *(right)*	600 – 800
163	Engraved goblet	600 – 800
164	Chris Lebeau bowl	500 – 800
165	Vase *(left)*	700 – 900
" "	Bowl *(right)*	500 – 700
166	Stipple engraved vase	2500 – 3500
167	Chargers (price for each)	400 – 500
168	Haussman vase *(left)*	1500 – 2000
" "	Haussman vase *(right)*	1200 – 1800
169	Royalit vase *(left)*	1200 – 1600
" "	Heliolit sugar bowl *(center)*	600 – 800
" "	Royalit vase *(right)*	1000 – 1300
169b	Royalit decanter and cordial set	2800 – 3200
170	Alexandrit vase *(upper left)*	600 – 800
" "	Alexandrit vase *(upper right)*	350 – 450
" "	Alexandrit dresser box *(lower left)*	500 – 600
" "	Alexandrit dresser box *(lower right)*	400 – 500
171	Splendid table service	N/P
172	Heliolit vase *(left)*	2200 – 2700
" "	Heliolit bowl *(center)*	2000 – 2500
" "	Heliolit compote *(right)*	800 – 1200
173	Presentation set	3500 – 4500

PLATE NO.	DESCRIPTION	EST. PRICE RANGE
174	Decanter set (with eight cordials)	$1200 – 1500
175	Decanter *(left)*	800 – 1200
" "	Decanter *(right)*	800 – 1200
176	Dresser box *(left)*	400 – 500
" "	Atomizer *(center)*	400 – 500
" "	Cologne bottle *(right)*	400 – 500
177	Presentation set	800 – 1200
178	Decanter	1000 – 1400
178b	Engraved vase *(top left)*	450 – 550
" "	Eldor vase *(center)*	350 – 450
" "	Cologne bottle *(top right)*	450 – 550
" "	Vase *(bottom left)*	250 – 350
" "	Cologne bottle *(bottom right)*	450 – 550
179	Wiener Werkstätte	N/P
180	Beryl Iris vase	N/P
181	Non rare-earth color samples	N/P
182	Bikava facet-cut vase	N/P
183	Bikava Corset vase	N/P
184	Beryl Sovereign vase	N/P
185	Sovereign vase	N/P
186	Rosalin Pedestal vase	N/P
187	Eldor facet-cut vase	N/P
188	Royalit Sovereign vase	N/P
189	Engraved Alexandrit decanter	1600 – 1800
190	Rosalin facet-cut Tulip vase	N/P
191	Facet-cut Hock wine goblets	N/P
192	Facet-cut Rosalin rose bowl	N/P
193	Engraved Hock wine goblets	N/P
194	Amethyst Sovereign facet-cut vase	N/P
195	Facet-cut Hock wine	N/P
196	Adolf Matura vase and bowl	N/P
197	Cut vase	N/P
198	Beaker *(left)*	300 – 400
" "	Vase *(right)*	350 – 450
199	Wine goblet *(left)*	1200 – 1500
" "	Cup and saucer *(right)*	800 – 1200
200	Shallow bowl *(left)*	600 – 800

PLATE NO.	DESCRIPTION	EST. PRICE RANGE
200	Cup and saucer *(right)*	$ 400 – 500
201	Decanters (price for each)	2500 – 3500
202	Pokal	6000 – 8000
203	Beaker	800 – 1200
204	Footed vase *(left)*	1200 – 1500
" "	Wine goblet *(center)*	500 – 700
" "	Decanter *(right)*	1800 – 2200
205	Cameo finger bowl and underplate *(left)*	500 – 800
" "	Finger bowl and underplate *(right)*	300 – 400
206	Wine goblet *(left)*	125 – 150
" "	Wine goblet *(center)*	125 – 150
" "	Wine goblet *(right)*	150 – 175
207	Cameo cordial goblet *(left)*	100 – 125
" "	Cameo dessert plate *(center)*	125 – 150
" "	Cameo sherbet and underplate	150 – 200
208	Malachite vase	350 – 450
209	Webb vase *(left)*	350 – 450
" "	Webb lidded vase *(right)*	800 – 1000
210	Webb vases *(left and right*; price for each)	400 – 600
" "	Webb vase *(center)*	800 – 1200
211	Webb bowl *(left)*	1200 – 1500
" "	Webb vase *(right)*	600 – 800
212	Harrach goblet	400 – 500
213	Harrach marquetry vase	350 – 450
214	Harrach marquetry cologne bottle	2500 – 3500
215	Moser juice glasses *(right and left*; price for each)	300 – 400
" "	Harrach vase *(center)*	350 – 450
216	Harrach vase	500 – 700
217	Harrach vase	300 – 500
218	Harrach vase	900 – 1200
219	Fritz Heckert vase	400 – 600
220	Cameo vase	300 – 400
221	Vase	1400 – 1800
222	Fritz Heckert chalice	1500 – 2000
223	Fritz Heckert pitcher	1200 – 1600
224	Fritz Heckert wine goblet *(left)*	250 – 350
" "	Fritz Heckert wine goblet *(right)*	600 – 800

PLATE NO.	DESCRIPTION	EST. PRICE RANGE
225	Fritz Heckert chalice *(left)*	$ 700 – 900
" "	Fritz Heckert vase *(right)*	350 – 450
226	Josephinenhütte ewer	1400 – 1800
227	Josephinenhütte loving cup	1200 – 1500
228	Josephinenhütte cup and saucer *(left)*	200 – 250
" "	Josephinenhütte wine goblet *(right)*	300 – 400
229	Rössler bowl	125 – 175
230	Riedel tall goblets *(left and right*; price for each)	1200 – 1600
" "	Riedel vase *(center)*	2500 – 3500
231	Riedel tankard	1500 – 1800
232	Löetz vase	400 – 500
233	Löetz vase	1200 – 1500
234	Löetz vase	500 – 700
235	Löetz vase *(left)*	1500 – 2000
" "	Löetz box *(right)*	1000 – 1200
236	Goldberg vase	300 – 400
237	Lidded container	300 – 400
238	Brocard goblet	600 – 800
239	Cameo-cut enameled vase	N/P
240	Mont Joye enameled vase	N/P
241	Sèvres jar	500 – 700
242	Decanter	3000 – 4000
243	Theresienthal römer	250 – 350
244	Theresienthal vase	400 – 600
245	Opaline vase *(left)*	350 – 450
" "	Biedermeier cologne *(center)*	900 – 1200
" "	Opaline cologne *(right)*	600 – 800

NOTES